WINSTON WHITE

Beyond
Conformity

The Free Press of Glencoe, Inc.

A DIVISION OF THE CROWELL-COLLIER PUBLISHING COMPANY

_28086

Acknowledgments

The extent to which I have drawn on the work of Talcott Parsons will be obvious in this book. I refer throughout to what he has written and I use his theoretical schemes to carry out my analysis. Less obvious are the many insights he personally gave me into the problems my topic has raised.

I also thank the following for their careful reading and perceptive criticism: Ian Davidson, Nathan Douthit, Janet Giele, W. Randall Huntsberry, David Riesman, Graham Stellwagon, and Robert W. White.

WINSTON WHITE

Dunster House,
Cambridge, Massachusetts
June, 1961

Contents

Contents

Beyond Conformity

1

Introduction

Since the end of World War II, intellectuals have expressed a growing concern about the quality of life in American society—particularly with what they believe to be a loss of individualism and a surrender to conformity. While others either point with pride to gains in the standard of living or worry for fear those gains have not been sufficiently rapid and extensive, the intellectuals question whether any such standard can be measured simply in terms of statistics on income and home-ownership, on goods consumed and jobs held. They know, of course, that these things are important. But more important to them is the very meaning of life in American society for the individual.

What good, they ask, are more cars and more homes in the suburbs if more Americans are losing their sense of purpose in life?—or worse, giving up thinking about it? What good are more television sets if what appears on their screens is trivial or degrading? What good is more income if it is spent on status-seeking and waste-making?

The intellectuals are worried about the impact of a highly bureaucratized and industrialized society on the individual. The individual, they believe, has become alienated, or cut off, from those relationships and experiences that once gave his life meaning and direction. They declare that he is no longer able or willing to find a way of life that would assert his essential humanity. The past, in failing to deliver what should have been the future, has given way instead to an amorphous present where the individual has lost his old goals and, with them, his sense of identity. The culture has lost its standards of excellence.

As the "togetherness" ethic of adjustment, or so the intellectuals tell us, replaces the old work ethic of achievement, individual greatness declines and man becomes a passive approval-seeker. Mass production shapes consumer taste, and mass media court the widest market through the lowest common denominator of appeal. Together they forge a mass culture whose vulgar banality undermines discrimination and crushes diversity. Mass culture seduces talent and breeds passivity, thus robbing the individual of his spontaneous creativity. Blind devotion to technology and science, they say, is leading us to a valueless disenchantment with the world that will usher in the brave new world of 1984, if indeed it is not already here.

These statements sum up what the intellectuals believe is going on—and going wrong—in American society. And, if we can judge from articles in magazines, sales of books, and reading assigned in college courses, their interpretation of the American condition is gaining an increasingly wide audience. In its way, this is all to the good. Americans, as Europeans are forever telling us, love to analyze themselves. But it is heartening, at least to this American, that they should choose to confront problems of such ultimate significance for the human condition, that they should ask whether their society or they themselves are to blame for what they believe is a failure to develop their human potentialities.

I do not, however, agree with the intellectuals' interpretation of what is happening. I think that an alternative interpretation is badly needed. Everyone agrees that American society has undergone rapid changes in the last decade and a half. Many of us, too, are deeply concerned about what these changes mean for the individual—how they affect the range of choices open to him, how they shape his own definition of life's purpose, what impact they have on the ways in which men live together in this imperfect world.

But the intellectuals, I believe, have failed to see the implications that these changes may have both for the individual and for the society. In general, their verdicts have been pessimistic jeremiads. My alternative interpretation is not necessarily optimistic, but it does try to redirect attention to what I believe are the real *challenges* that are emerging. It also tries to explain why other interpretations have failed to recognize these changes and challenges properly.

These changes, as I see them, create new opportunities for the individual to choose for himself rather than impose limitations upon him. And they are challenges because they make new demands on the individual—demands that he has never before had to face in quite the same way. He is now confronted with choices and with the necessity of understanding their complex nature for which his previous experience is not an adequate guide. In fact, it is the intellectuals' particular type of reference to previous experience that leads them to misinterpret the changes that have obviously occurred. They tend, for example, to analyze the noneconomic problems of the present in terms of the economic problems of the past. I am attempting, then, to redefine the problems that the individual in American society is facing.

To do this requires an analysis of American society—at least in those respects that will concern us here. Accordingly, my purpose is to analyze what the intellectuals have to say as an *ideology*—that is, an interpretation of the way things are in society made by those who share some particular conception of the way things ought to be—and to indicate where I believe this ideology is limited and, indeed, wrong.

This chapter will be addressed to the necessary academic task of defining the terms "intellectual" and "ideology" and of explaining what is involved in analyzing an ideology.

The Intellectuals

Our use of the term "intellectuals" does not refer to all intellectuals in general. Intellectuals in general may be thought of as trustees of the society's cultural heritage who seek to preserve and transmit it and to explore and develop alternatives to the existing tradition. Sometimes they are simply defined as men who work with and for ideas.

Our particular group, however, performs a more special function. Through teaching, preaching, and writing, they warn society when they think it is deserting the standards of its heritage or failing to develop those alternatives that would enrich it. They are *social critics*. In addition to describing the actual state of affairs in the society, they also judge it. They diagnose weaknesses and prescribe cures. They editorialize as well as report.

Another characteristic is their independence. As critics, they are primarily interested in the relevance of ideas to solving society's problems. They are not directly concerned with serving any particular interest-group or organization. In Karl Mannheim's words, they transform "conflicts of interest into conflicts of ideas" (Coser, 1956a, p. 116). They are, if you will, free-lance thinkers.

Finally, although the problems that elicit their attention may lead them to focus on particular aspects of the situation, they do not limit their discourse to any particular field but explore the entire area for relevance to the problems at hand. They eschew the limitations of specialization. They are likely to be literary men—authors, critics, free-lance writers or journalists. But there is a considerable overlap into the academic world and among them we find humanists, historians, theologians, sociologists, and economists; men who escape the confines of their disciplines from time to time to take the larger view.

The lines dividing our intellectuals from the academicians are far from clearly drawn, particularly within the sociological profession. First, many of the ideological issues raised deal with topics that are also the subject of sociological investigation. Second, many of the questions that sociologists are seeking to answer are being asked for the first time from the perspective of social science. As a relatively new field, sociology is bound to be shot through with ideological assumptions as well as issues.

Intellectual Ideology as a Topic of Investigation.—However debatable the adequacy of sociological knowledge may be, sociological theory and knowledge have advanced sufficiently so that it is perhaps not premature to bring it to bear on some of the ideological issues current today—in particular, those raised by the intellectuals. In this essay, we will be asking, what have they to say about what is going on in American society and about the condition of American culture? What evidence have they adduced? How do they interpret it? What underlying assumptions have they made? We will then assess their assumptions and interpretations in the light of available sociological knowledge and offer an alternative interpretation.

I have established the content of the intellectual ideology by a systematic reading of five periodicals—*American Scholar, Atlantic Monthly, Commentary, Dissent,* and *Partisan Review.* Articles were selected from issues published from 1949 through 1958 with the exception of *Dissent,* which started publication in 1954. I looked for articles about American society and culture where the author was criticizing the state of affairs, where he was primarily interested in confronting what he regarded as a problem, where he was not a spokesman for a particular interest-group, and where he directed his attention to the implications of the problem for the total society. Thus, articles dealing with specific issues were not included unless those issues led to the consideration of broader areas of concern.

The five periodicals were selected after sampling about a thousand pages from each of fifteen periodicals that seemed the most likely channels for intellectuals.

These five will no doubt strike many as an incongruous assortment. The reader of the so-called "highbrow" *Partisan Review* may be astonished to find his magazine in the company of the "middlebrow" *Atlantic Monthly;* the avowedly radical *Dissent* might very well consider it a lack of discrimination to be included with such magazines as *Commentary* and *American Scholar.* Yet despite differences of approach, in these five magazines were found most of the articles by intellectuals as social critics. There were, of course, differences in interpretation, but the broad issue of conformity and mass culture was generally common to them all. And, with some exceptions, the conclusion reached was that the current situation is cause for alarm. In the discussion that follows in Chapter 2, I will discriminate among the various ideological backgrounds represented, but I will not be concerned with drawing distinctions among editorial policies. Nor, for that matter, will I suggest that the point of view I am discussing is the only one to be found in these periodicals. In addition, relevant material from other sources will be used when the point of view expressed is along similar lines.

The Problem of Ideology

An ideology is a selective interpretation of the state of affairs in society made by those who share some particular conception of what it ought to be. For obvious enough reasons that will be spelled out as we go along, there is always a discrepancy between the way things are and the way they ought to be—a discrepancy that sociologist Talcott Parsons calls *strain* (1951, *passim*). Since strain does not affect every member or group in the society in the same way, the same strain will produce a variety of reactions. In addition, these reactions to strain may take a variety of forms—conflict, aggression, apathy, discontent. An ideology is *one* type of reaction to strain. It is usually a formulation of beliefs about the source of strain and what should be done to eliminate it, although sometimes it can take the form of a denial that there is any strain at all and an assertion that "all's right in the world."

Values and Conditions.—The crux of our analysis here lies in the conception of strain—the relation between the way things ought to be and the way they are; or between *values* and *conditions*. Values, to paraphrase Kluckhohn (1952, p.

395), are conceptions of the desirable (what ought to be desired as opposed to what is simply desired whether it ought to be or not). Values are standards by which things are judged as being better or worse than one another. They are conceptions of what a *good* thing ought to be—a good society, a good person, a good law—and of what are good choices when one is faced with alternative courses of action.

Making choices or taking action, however, has other aspects than evaluation. No matter how desirable a particular choice may be, it cannot be carried out without taking into account other requirements than simply implementing the desirable. The ideal has to come to terms with limitations in the real world, with the "facts of life." Since there is always a gap between the ideal and the real, strain is inevitable. Ideology is an effort to close that gap.

The values of a society are rooted in its cultural heritage, including its religious background. Inherent in the latter are conceptions of the meaning of man's life on earth, of his relation to other men and to himself, and of his relation to nature. For any society, therefore, values will include a conception of what a good society ought to be like. Certain social patterns of men's relationships to each other will be preferred and will be considered the most desirable way of carrying out the more general cultural values.

But this conception of what the good society ought to be like cannot be realized without coming to terms with conditions inherent in social organization. The organization of society requires that the relationships among its members be arranged so that economic resources—at the least, a minimum of food, clothing, and shelter—are produced and distributed, political order is maintained, children are reared and trained to assume adult responsibilities, and the like. All of these conditions are to be found in *any* society no matter what its values are. While values are exceedingly important in determining the way in which those conditions will be met, they do not in themselves supply specific solutions. Simply put, values may tell you what ought to be done, but they do not tell you how to do it. They do not tell you, for example, *how* to curb inflation or prevent famine.

To illustrate the complexities of social conditions more fully, let us take a specific example. Let us say that, in terms of the cultural and religious heritage, life on earth is considered a good thing, that the dignity of man as an individual is highly esteemed, and that a good life for man is considered to be one in which he masters his environment and turns its resources toward improving his lot. The good society which could attain these desirable things might be conceived of as one that, among other considerations, provides a high standard of living for its members. But before this can be accomplished, a vast range of conditions must be met.

Of what does a high standard of living consist? How are available resources to be allocated among housing, clothing, food, recreation, education, etc.? Is the production of these items to be privately or publicly managed, or both? Should the standard of living vary from one individual to another in terms of his contribution? If so, how does one assess the contribution? Should resources be withheld from raising the present standard of living in order to be plowed back into capital so that future standards may be higher? To what extent should the realization of a high standard impinge on other desirable things, like the defense of the nation, the protection of individual freedom of choice, and so on?

Clearly, coming to terms with this array of conditions— and these are but a few—and reconciling them with each other is a source of strain. The degree of strain in any case will vary from one part of the society to another and from time to time. It is likely to reach greater proportions during periods of rapid social change. Those who perceive strain in the same way *and*, most important, who share similar beliefs about its remedy, may react to it by formulating an ideological interpretation of its cause and cure (or by subscribing to what others have formulated).

Interest: Advantage or Concern?—Discussions in sociological literature often identify those who share certain ideological perceptions and beliefs as an *interest* group—a group identifiable by their social, political, or economic position in society whom strain affects in the same way and whose interest is to resolve it to their advantage. A strain that has its source, for instance, in the problems of allocating corporate income or in government regulation of corporate activities will affect the interests of businessmen differently from the way that it affects members of a labor union. Each group will perceive strain according to its own interests. Marx, for example, claimed that perception according to interests was relative to the class-position of the perceiver. Although these interests undoubtedly determine ideological reactions to an important extent, the latter are by no means a clear-cut reflection of the former. People with interests in common do not necessarily agree with one another in their analysis of what constitutes a threat to their interests or of how they should be protected. Interests are certainly an important determinant of ideological reaction, but they are not the only one.

Just as every individual has some sort of psychological "theory," whether he knows it or not, that enables him to make some sense out of his own actions and those of others, so do members of a society have some sort of social "theory" about the way their society functions. They interpret what goes on in the society and make decisions on the basis of such a social "theory." Even a decision *not* to decide is based on some sort of implicit premises. When an individual who does not vote in an election says, "My vote doesn't count anyway, so why bother?" he is expressing his interpretation of the way he thinks his society operates.

These attitudes and assumptions, these "theories," are shaped by other determinants besides that of any one particular interest. Psychological differences among individuals, differences in personal experiences and in sources of information, conflicts among a variety of interests acting on the same person, all determine interpretations of social events. Thus, any particular ideological reaction may catch up in its net groups of people with *varying* interests, unless one wants to say that they have an "interest" in common of subscribing to the same ideology. The difficulty here is a semantic one. When one speaks of an interest group, he is using the word interest to mean *advantage,* or benefit; when he speaks of an interest in a problem, he means special attention, or *concern.*

The analysis of why any particular assortment of persons, or even social types of persons, are resonant to the same ideology is, then, exceedingly more complex than simply saying that they all share a desire to protect advantages in common. In analyzing the ideology of the intellectuals, we will be mainly concerned with the social "theories" on which their assumptions about society and man's relation to it are based. And we will be able to say something about why the intellectuals embrace these particular ideas, but our approach will not be primarily in terms of their vested interests in their social status. If we can speak of vested interests at all, it will be mainly in terms of the intellectuals' desire to protect their ideas for the sake of themselves, not because doing so yields economic, political, or social advantage. Although this attitude is related to the intellectuals' characteristic of "independence" mentioned earlier, interest in ideas for their own sake is not exclusive to intellectuals. Although intellectuals are perhaps more aware of this commitment than others, other groups also cling tenaciously to their ideas for their own sake, albeit often without realizing it. Indeed, many groups often seem to act as if they preferred sinking with their ideas intact rather than revising their customary way of looking at the world.

Selectivity and Distortion.—Ideology becomes a problem because an analysis of society is attempted by its own members. Objectivity is more difficult in the study of social phenomena than in the study of physical phenomena because the investigator is himself involved in what he is analyzing. What he has to say will very likely be unintentionally selective in that he will choose only those aspects of the situation that seem important to him and he will play down or ignore others. The way in which a strain affects him and the nature of the assumptions (his social "theory") he brings to bear on its interpretation will determine the questions he thinks are important.

His particular point of view, then, will not only tend to predetermine the answers to the questions he does ask but will also lead him to omit important questions he should have asked. Louis Wirth has said, "The most important thing, therefore, that we can know about a man is what he takes for granted . . ." (Mannheim, 1936, pp. xxii-xxiii). Similarly, the most important thing we can know about an ideologist is what he assumes, what he thinks unimportant, what he is unaware of.

Ideological selectivity leads into distortion when statements made on the basis of only these selected aspects purport to account as well for the neglected aspects (Parsons, 1961). The distinction between ideological selectivity and distortion involves the level of generality at which the statement is made: a statement that is selective at a specific level becomes distortion when made at a more general level. To say, for instance, that many men in industrial society have lost their freedom to choose what hours to work and what specific tasks to perform is true at a specific level. But to say, on the basis of this observation, that men have lost their freedom in general is distortion since it ignores other areas in which greater freedom of choice has been gained. Another type of distortion is found in statements that can be shown to be a misrepresentation of the known facts in the case. Sometimes distortion is the product of sheer fantasy.

The application of available social scientific knowledge is the means for demonstrating ideological selectivity and distortion. The knowledge of questions known to be significant and of answers known to be validated can be used for pointing out the questions that an ideology has failed to ask and for correcting the answers it has distorted. It is not necessary that social science reach perfection before such an analysis is attempted, for the problem is a relative one—pointing out the discrepancy between ideological beliefs and what is currently known to be significant and correct. Of course, social science, as well as *all* knowledge, is itself selective in that we obviously do not know everything there is to know. Our knowledge is limited not only by the means of investigation available to us but, perhaps more importantly, by the kinds of questions any of us ask of our data. With the accumulation of knowledge, succeeding generations of investigators ask questions that never occurred to their predecessors.

Selectivity, however, is not an all-or-none affair. It is itself relative; it can be present in greater or less degree. Thus, no matter how selective available knowledge may be, ideology is by definition even *more* selective in that it omits considerations that knowledge has already established as significant (cf. Parsons, 1961). What is currently known can be used to demonstrate this omission by accounting for observable data that an ideological interpretation is unable to explain.

Independence of Content from Source.—In analyzing the content of the intellectuals' ideology, we will be concerned with assessing the validity of the answers they have given to the questions they have asked and, particuarly, with looking for the questions that they failed to ask at all. But we will follow this procedure solely on the basis of what is sociologically relevant for the analysis of American society. We will not be able to discredit their statements on the basis of their motives for making them, because the validity of what a person has to say is not necessarily a direct reflection of his motives for saying it. People with the best of intentions *can* make invalid statements; people with the most ulterior motives *can* speak the truth. If an insane person, for example, says that it is raining outside, we might suspect the validity of his statement. But the only way we can test its validity is to look outside and see if it is actually raining.

A statement, therefore, cannot be refuted simply by discrediting the person making it in an *ad-hominem* manner, by "unmasking his motives," as Mannheim put it (1936, p. 39). One cannot discredit the statements of a businessman or a Marxist simply by saying, "Look who's talking!" This type of "refutation" is common enough in ideological disputes and we shall try to avoid it.

One more caution in this respect. Since we judge content independently of its source, we do not, of course, assume that every statement made by someone outside of the social sciences is *ipso facto* ideological. Selectivity and distortion in the content must be demonstrated. The social scientist can claim no monopoly on being the only competent observer. Equally important, neither can he assume that every statement made by other social scientists is *ipso facto not* ideological. He must apply scientific standards to content whatever its source.

Preview

These general comments on ideology will be illustrated in the analysis of our present case—the intellectuals' ideology. It is to be remembered that when we use the word "intellectuals," we are speaking only of certain spokesmen among intellectuals in general. We are not investigating the extent to which their opinions are shared either by the rest of the intellectual community or by the population as a whole. In addition, we are analyzing an ideological viewpoint, not the editorial policies of the periodicals from which we derived much of our material or the beliefs of particular individuals, although our analysis will necessarily entail focussing on particular spokesmen whose statements are considered to be representative of the ideology.

Chapters 2-5 will set forth the content of the intellectuals' ideology—their description of what they think is happening in American society and their evaluation of it. Chapters 6, 7, and 8 will offer an alternative interpretation based on available sociological knowledge in terms of which we will point out the selectivity and distortion in the ideology and attempt to arrive at a more accurate assessment of the situation. Chapter 9 will investigate some of the reasons that have led the intellectuals to make their imputations about American society and to react in the way they have. This investigation will be made in terms of their perception of strain and the way in which it has shaped those imputations. Finally, Chapter 10 will discuss some of the positive consequences ideology may have both for the society and for social science. In particular, this chapter will examine the role of the intellectual as an agent of ideas.

The Content
of Intellectual Ideology

2

Two Approaches
to Cause and Cure

When more than a hundred observers writing in five magazines comment on the state of American society, they are
bound—despite the common focus of their concern—to come
up with different interpretations and varied emphases. But
if there is one issue on which they conform with one another,
it is that of conformity. Whenever the individual finds himself in a group, our commentators tell us, be it in the office
or over the barbecue pit, he wants to fit in and be accepted;
like Willy Loman, he wants not only to be liked but to be
well-liked. He strives for this by being sensitive to what the
rest of the group considers acceptable standards of behavior
(other-direction) and acts accordingly; in short, he conforms.
Since in conforming, he is careful not to do or say anything that will rub the *others* the wrong way, the idiosyncratic rough edges of *his* personality are rubbed away; in
consequence, he becomes scarcely distinguishable from those
whose approbation he seeks.

Nor does he have the option of behaving differently, for
the others operate on the same premises and judge him in
terms of them; there is social pressure for conformity. Given
this way of looking at the problem, the issue is clearly drawn:
it is one of the individual *versus* society (variously conceived
as peer-group, work-team, bureaucracy, etc.). On the one
hand, society must ensure some degree of conformity from
its members; on the other, the individual must have the

opportunity to choose for himself and to become himself. The question is seen as one of conflict, as a choice between either taking sides or reconciling them in some sort of compromise. The individual, presumably, can choose between the extremes of being a beatnik or an organization man, can compromise somewhere in between, or he can follow Riesman's suggestion and strive for autonomy by rendering unto society a tongue-in-cheek conformity while searching for the loopholes that have not yet been plugged up. "The problem," says Dennis Wrong, "of where the individual *ends* and society *begins* . . . is a perennial one for the social sciences [my italics]" (1956, p. 333), as indeed it has been for the history of Western thought.

However hoary the problem may be, I see it as the central concern underlying current intellectual ideology. Murray Hausknecht sums it up:

When we talk of the pressures for conformity we are saying in effect that it is increasingly difficult for individuals to bring their own distinctive styles to their social roles. We are saying that it is becoming harder to seize upon the ambiguities which pervade all spheres of action and use them to explore other alternatives, because the disciplines [of social control] are being so narrowed as to eliminate these ambiguities. (1957, p. 57)

Other commentators go on to suggest that the pressure for conformity reaches beyond behavior in groups to permeate the very structure of both personality and culture. Since society allegedly needs smooth co-operators that fit in without friction (Fromm, 1955-56), man becomes a cog in the machine; his feeling of identity becomes reduced to "*I am as you desire me*" (Fromm, 1947, p. 73). The personality no longer internalizes definitive goals but rather the process, and "*only the process . . . itself*" (Riesman, 1950, p. 22), of seeking guidance from others. Similarly, popular culture, in anticipatory socialization, trains men how to behave now so that adjustment to "a future nightmare" will be easier (Hausknecht, 1957, p. 57). Even religion has been pressed into service. A Unitarian minister asserts that the so-called religious revival is a search not for faithful commitment to transcendent values but for a palliative in the "gospel of smooth adjustment" (Meserve, 1955, p. 35).

Intellectuals agree in this respect not only about the way things are but also about the way they ought to be. Conformity and the pressures for it are seen as excessive, for they stifle the development of the individual's uniqueness; not only his choice among alternative paths of action but even his awareness of those available is restricted. It should not be overlooked that this state of affairs could have been evaluated as a highly desirable one of unprecedented social harmony, but where the issue is conceived of as an either-or choice, the intellectuals are clearly on the side of the individual. Underlying this position is the strong emphasis on individualism in the American system of values itself. That this same emphasis is common to the business creed as well illustrates the point made previously that ideologies share with each other a common framework of values, even though their interpretations differ.

Larger than the issue of conformity itself is the depiction of an all-pervasive leveling, a narrowing—if not the complete elimination—of all differences in every aspect of American society. As partly cause, partly consequence of conformity, the disappearance of distinctions among individuals applies as well to differences among age groups, classes, regions, even to those between the sexes. The hierarchical differences between parent and child, teacher and pupil, boss and employee dwindle as the authority of the superior becomes transformed into the manipulation of a pal. Differences among classes dwindle, "for with the growth of the new middle class the older, hierarchical patterns disintegrate, and it is not easy to compare ranks among the several sets of hierarchies that do exist" (Riesman, 1950, p. 48).

Returning from a year in London, Dwight Macdonald dramatizes the sorry pass things have come to in America, where everybody is " 'equal' in the sense that nobody respects anybody else unless he has to, by *force majeure*" (1958a, p.

315). Things are different over there [in England]; there
"each person [is] differentiated by status and function but
each a part of an orderly social structure."

Edward Sapir found a "flat cultural morass . . . geographi-
cally widespread," the culture itself one of "little depth or
individuality to begin with."

To find substantially the same cultural manifestations, material and
spiritual, often indeed to the minutest details, in New York and
Chicago and San Francisco is saddening. It argues a shallowness in
the culture itself and a readiness to imitation in its bearers that is
not reassuring. (Sapir, 1949, p. 330)

Perhaps most fundamentally threatening is the alleged
erosion of sex differences, as men "lose" their masculinity;
women, their femininity. The American male, once hardy,
vigorous, and unflattering (Richter, 1950), has become a
yes-man to both wife and employer. The American woman,
who once knew that father was master, is now hard, dominat-
ing, and holds men's job—not to mention sitting at their
bars. As models of identity for their children, both perpetuate the lack of differentiation.

Hand in hand with the issue of conformity and of equal
salience is that of mass culture. Intellectuals find Sapir's
cultural morass equally flat and widespread throughout the
"cultural" content that is mass-produced by mass media for
mass audiences. Mass culture, says Dwight Macdonald,

. . . is a dynamic, revolutionary force, breaking down the old barriers
of class, tradition, taste, and dissolving all cultural distinctions. It
mixes and scrambles everything together, producing what might be
called homogenized culture, after another American achievement, the
homogenization process that distributes the globules of cream evenly
throughout the milk instead of allowing them to float separately on
top. It thus destroys all values, since value judgments imply discrimination. Mass culture is very, very democratic: it absolutely refuses to
discriminate against, or between, anything or anybody. All is grist
to its mill, and all comes out finely ground indeed. (1957, p. 62)

Closely related to the homogenization of culture is taste in
consumers' goods; persuaded by admen—whose methods if
not themselves were hidden before the revelations of Vance

Packard (1957)—to want things they do not need or "really" want, millions of Americans buy identical products, at best only marginally differentiated.

For the present, I am concerned only with outlining the *symptoms* of strain that intellectuals detect in American society—an area in which there is considerable consensus. In general, the picture is one of a leveling of distinctions— of homogenization, to use Macdonald's term. On one side, the individual is being squeezed and—because of his conformity—allowing himself to be squeezed; on the other, social pressures and mass culture are doing the squeezing. It is, in effect, a picture of the mass society. If we take Riesman's formula for the link between the individual and society as one where the society must ensure some degree of conformity from its members and where the individual seeks meaningful guidance from the society, we have what could be described as a "runaway inflationary" process where the customers are all too eager to buy any "goods" that are offered, and where the "goods" are being sold by high-pressure techniques. The picture looks something like this:

$$\text{Individuals} \quad \overset{\text{excessive conformity}}{\underset{\text{excessive regulation}}{\rightleftarrows}} \quad \text{"Society"}$$

Two Approaches to Cause and Cure

In the preceding chapter, we noted that ideology is one type of reaction to strain in the society. Strain was defined as the discrepancy between *what ought to be* and *what is*, between values and their implementation in society. Values are conceptions of the desirable. They formulate some notion of what ought to be. Social conditions present problems as to how the values can be implemented, problems for which the values cannot by themselves supply specific solutions. Simply put, a value may tell you what ought to be done, but it doesn't tell you how to do it. Conditions in the society raise problems that go beyond simply attaining the desirable. The essential question is, "To what extent does a given social structure facilitate (or impede) the implementation of values?" The focus, then, of ideological issues lies in the relation between *values* and the *conditions of social structure*.

This relation provides an exceedingly useful dimension on which to classify ideologies. Ideologies, we have seen, are selective. In one way, they are selective by emphasizing only one side of the value-social structure relation (Geertz, 1957).

A value-oriented ideology asserts that strain is primarily the result of a weakening of the values on which the society is based. It recommends that these basic values be reasserted and appeals to "higher levels," such as "the American way of life," "the glory of France," "the Western heritage." It seeks to strengthen these values at the various structural levels so that they may be more effective guides in controlling social conditions, such as institutional arrangements. It emphasizes what are sometimes called "ideal factors"—values, morals, beliefs, and the like. Such an ideology tends to be *moralistic*, naïve about structural conditions (although this naïvete may have the unintended consequence of accepting them as they are), and vague about specific programs.

A social structure-oriented ideology sees strain as primarily the result of unsatisfactory social conditions. It recommends that these be *reformed* (*re-formed*), and it appeals to the "hard realities" of the situation. It seeks to improve these conditions so that they may more effectively realize the values, which are *not* seen as problematical. It emphasizes what are called "real factors"—things like political and economic institutions, power and property. This type of ideology tends to be sophisticated about conditions (although this may backfire if it means pressing for too drastic, hence unacceptable, change) and specific about programs.

This distinction between value-oriented and structure-oriented ideologies is useful in analyzing the intellectual case—where the consensus on symptoms and on evaluation of them is accompanied by differences in diagnoses of the causes of the symptoms and in recommendations of what is to be done. If we look at the issue as one of deficient individual freedom and development and excessive social pressure, we can discern two main streams: each one offers a different explanation of "whose fault it is."

One stream of thought is value-oriented and places the blame on individuals. It sees the present undesirable state of affairs as primarily due to their defection; individuals have become slack about living up to basic values, if not guilty of deserting them altogether. We need a reassertion of value-commitments by individuals. People are urged, for example, to reaffirm the (American) value of individualism and "not to conform," although what lines non-conformity should take are usually left unspecified; for, naturally, specification might hamper individual styles of non-conformity. It is left to the individual whether he should throw out his television set, grow a beard, or tell the boss off. Analysis in this case tends to follow a "humanistic" tone. For purposes of easier reference, I shall call those who share the value-oriented ideology *moralizers*.

The moralizers may or may not diagnose the structural conditions that have contributed to society's strain; but whatever the conditions are alleged to be, they are regarded as given—that is, not many structures can or should be changed. The emphasis here is on strengthening the underlying values that guide individual action within existing structures.

We may anticipate some conceptual difficulties at this point. Since various ideological statements use different terms, it is likely to be confusing when we try to compare and order them. The following discussion, however, may be more consistent than is apparent if it is kept in mind that values are conceptions of the desirable—the "oughts"—that in part determine the choices people make. Thus, terms like individualism, Protestant ethic, inner-direction, and the like express, among other things, criteria of what one ought to do.

The other stream of thought is social structure-oriented and places the blame for strain on social conditions. According to this version, the very structure of society itself prevents its members from developing their potentialities and from realizing the good life. Economic and political institutions, bureaucracy, and mass culture are such that no one could be expected to transcend their deadening clutch. What is needed is *structural reform*—the elimination of advertising or of middlebrow entertainment, of bureaucracy or of capitalism in general. This is necessary to release the potentialities of individuals, whose value commitments would have expressed themselves spontaneously had they not been corrupted by structural conditions. Analysis along these lines tends to follow a "sociological" tone. Those who share this point of view I shall refer to as *reformers*.

Reinhold Niebuhr, although talking in a slightly different context, has hit on the two types of emphasis discussed here:

The liberal world has always oscillated between the [structure-oriented] hope of creating perfect men by eliminating the social sources of evil and the [value-oriented] hope of so purifying human "reason" by educational techniques [in this case, ideological exhortation] that all social institutions would gradually become the bearers of a universal human will, informed by a universal human mind. (1952, p. 68)

The following three chapters will set forth these two main branches of the intellectual ideology. I will quote not only from the five periodicals whose articles in this area form the basis for determining the ideological content but also from other sources that develop the same themes. Most of the outside sources are writings by the same people who contributed to the periodicals. Although the framework for the discussion of the statements about American society is my own, the statements themselves represent the views of the intellectuals. Thus these chapters will define the intellectual's interpretation of American society, and I will reserve critical comment for the subsequent chapters, which will present my alternative interpretation.

Obviously, not all of the intellectuals quoted in this section would agree with every statement made by other intellectuals; some take more extreme positions than others. A few are neither predominantly moralizers nor reformers but a mixture. In fairness, I will distinguish wherever possible among different approaches to the same topic—but it is essential to bear in mind that I am concerned with sorting out different types of approaches, or sets of ideas, rather than with distinguishing among the authors themselves. The reference point throughout is what is said about American society. This is not an analysis of individual ideologists or of periodicals. It is an analysis of ideology.

3

The Moralizers' Approach

. . . the American citadel is *a* man. Not man in general. Not man in
the abstract. Not the majority of men. But man. *That* man. *His*
worth. *His* uniqueness. (MacLeish, 1951b, p. 27)

Thus Archibald MacLeish states in its purest humanistic
form the case for individualism, for the "freedom of the
individual human being to think for himself and to come
to the truth by the light of his own mind and conscience, . . .
[*not*] freedom to be like everybody else" (1951b, p. 27).
(Just as many discussions of American society start with
Tocqueville, so does the word *individualism*, although he
spoke of it in somewhat unflattering terms. See *Democracy
in America*, vol. 2, p. 104.)

Appealing to the national past, MacLeish reminds us that
the faith in freedom, in man, was a belief at the base of the
American republic, subscribed to by the Founding Fathers
(some of whom, by the way, had serious reservations about
the irresponsibility of the masses). This faith, he asserts, has
been deserted; there has been instead a "massive, almost
glacial shift away from the passion for individual freedom
and toward a desire for security of association, of belonging,
of conformity" (1953, p. 398). As e. e. cummings puts it,
". . . nowadays, I see people who've been endowed with
legs crawling on their chins after quote security unquote"
(1953b, p. 53).

The verdict is *loss of the old values*. We have fallen from
a state of grace, if you will. In the past, the sacredness of
human life was anchored in certainties of one form or another, says Krutch, in notions of the soul, God, free will,

and the unique personality (1956). These certainties have been so undermined that "things can't go on this way much longer" (Krutch, 1953, p. 142).

Means and Ends; Science and Values.—Why have these values been deserted? The reference, as is characteristic of a value-oriented ideology, is again to a "higher level"—this time to what has happened in the realm of ideas (at the cultural level): *the knowledge of means has undermined the commitment to ends.* No wonder there has been a "tragic loss of heart," asserts MacLeish (1953, p. 398), in an age when schoolboys are taught only techniques and know nothing of the "great conceptions of human destiny." Science and technology are the principal malefactors, for their rationale is one of the pursuit of perfection without purpose (Walter Marx, 1949, p. 392).

Science can do much, Krutch says, but it cannot decide what it *ought* to do; it has deprived us of premises that might have made us feel capable of deciding: "we have educated ourselves out of certain ideas necessary to our survival" (1953, p. 150). Either we know more than is good for us, Krutch thinks, or we know less about man than about matter. The trouble may be, he adds, in studying man as if he were a machine, a dog, or a rat.

MacLeish, after defining the tragedy of our time as the preoccupation with means and the loss of concern with ends, explains how science has helped bring about this state of affairs. Knowledge by science, he reminds us, is through abstractions; but, he adds, you can't know reality, facts, things, by abstractions: ". . . nothing can be known through an abstraction but the abstraction itself . . . all true knowledge is a matter of relation . . . our relation with it" (1956, p. 50). Somewhat more willing to give the devil his due, Douglas Bush follows concession with warning:

Science and scientific method are of course essential parts of a liberal education, but there seems to be increasing danger that science and technology will swallow up everything else. Nothing has been commoner of late years than the demand that, in this age, we need more and more science in education. It may be doubted if the cure for delirium tremens is brandy. It is not being hostile to science to say, as many scientists have said, that in an age dominated by science and technology we need more of the humanities. (1959, p. 2)

Bush asserts that the humanities will help bring about a reassertion of values on the part of individuals:

The aim of the humanities is not to adjust people to life, to the pressures and the low ideals of mass civilization, but to enlighten and disturb them, to strengthen them to adjust life and themselves to the traditional ideals of the best minds, the saving remnant of the human race. (1959, p. 3)

The moralizers are not particularly concerned with the influence of science and technology on social structures (a salient issue with the reformers); their uneasiness arises, rather, from the belief that preoccupation with scientific and technological means may very likely undermine the evaluative bases of action. They are concerned with what they see as an ideological, even pseudo-religious trust in science itself as an implicit magic that will apotropaically ward off evil and guarantee "success" in reaching desired ends with no thought of their desirability. Science, they fear, has become modern man's sacred cow: the vitamin replaces the crucifix; the tranquilizer reconciles man to God's ways. Advertising, says Marshall McLuhan, encourages us to believe that every human failure can be overcome by the "scientifically certified formula. . . . The fault is not in our stars but our jars that we are underlings" (1957, p. 441).

With the mastery of nuclear fission and of outer space, man is seen as arrogantly violating both the microscopic and macroscopic limits of his worldly existence. In either playing-God or playing-with-Nature, man is undermining the very basis of the meaning of his life on earth. Hannah Arendt, in *The Human Condition*, develops this theme at length:

. . . we look and live in this society as though we were as far removed from our own human existence as we are from the infinitely small and the immensely large which, even if they could be perceived by the finest instruments, are too far away from us to be experienced. (1958, p. 323)

Our experiences of "worldliness," she says, "escape more and more the range of ordinary human experience" (p. 323) so that the hallmark of the modern age is world-alienation (p. 254). In a review of Robert Jungk's *Tomorrow Is Already Here*, Arthur Ray quotes Jungk as saying that America's reaching for omnipotence and trying to win absolute mastery over nature undermine the national ethos. America is trying to "become God":

> Freedom and humanity fall by the wayside. What is needed, says Jungk, is a "great spiritual change which would have to express itself in the recognition once again of human limits and the rediscovery of moderation." (Ray, 1955, p. 69)

In undermining the values that might hold them in check, science and technology are feared for their potentiality to become the sole criteria of human behavior, crushing man in the process. Like the sorcerer's apprentice, man has summoned up powers he cannot restrain. He is doomed to tend the machine he invented, as in Butler's *Erewhon*.

Most alarming of all, it is said, is the presumption that there can be a "science" of human behavior—a social science of man. There are two mutually exclusive points of view on this topic—often entertained simultaneously. One is that a science of man is not possible; the other is that such a science is not only possible but will lead to the manipulation of human beings with the road paved (however good the intentions) to Huxley's or Orwell's hell-on-earth. Jungk's title suggests that we have already arrived.

William Whyte, avoiding the fallacy of embracing both points of view at once, thinks that Jungk's "tomorrow" will probably never arrive. He shares, however, the fear that false trust in science—what he calls "scientism"—will lead us to surrender to powers that cannot deliver what they promise. Advertising, public relations, psychological tests—in short, social engineering—will be unable to deliver the millenium:

> What I am arguing is that the real impact of scientism is upon our values. The danger, to put it another way, is not man being dominated but man surrendering. [Again, values and their assertion by

the individual are the focus.] At the present writing there is not one section of American life that has not drunk deeply of the promise of scientism. It appears in many forms—pedagogy, aptitude tests, that monstrous nonentity called "mass communication" and there are few readers who have not had a personal collision with it. (Whyte, 1956, p. 35)

"Decline of the Protestant Ethic" and "Togetherness."— What has happened to the individual in this alleged state of affairs (and what describes his part in bringing it about) can perhaps be summed up by these chapter-titles from Whyte's best-seller, *The Organization Man.* MacLeish (as quoted) referred to an "almost glacial shift away from the passion for individual freedom and toward the desire for security of association, of belonging, of conformity"; Whyte offers an explanation. The very basis of American values— the Protestant Ethic of hard work, self-reliance, thrift, and the pursuit of individual salvation—has given way to what Whyte calls the social ethic. The social ethic has three major propositions:

. . . a belief in the group as the source of creativity; a belief in "belongingness" as the ultimate need of the individual; and a belief in the application of science to achieve the belongingness. (1956, p. 7)

Not putting all the blame on the individual, Whyte points out structural changes that have made the Protestant Ethic out-of-date. With the growth of large organizations, the self-reliance of "rugged individualism" has given way to the "co-operation" of administrators; thrift has been replaced by pension plans and is even discouraged from the fear that consumption will lag behind production. People have been led to believe that the necessities of working and getting along together in the group are of such importance that they look upon individual initiative and competition as factors disruptively rocking the boat.

Whyte aims his main battery toward the group. "The central fallacy, I believe, lies in what can be called false collectivization" (1956, p. 55). First, he says, there is an over-emphasis on morale instead of task-accomplishment; second, a group does not create because "people very rarely *think* in groups, they talk together, they exchange information" (p. 57); third, the fear of authoritarianism has turned into fear of leadership. The result? A leaderless group of "co-operators" who look with suspicion on the man with ideas (the non-conformist), who look with suspicion even on their *own* ideas for fear that expressing them will arouse hostility and who then feel guilty for keeping quiet (pp. 61-6).

But having acknowledged the structural changes, Whyte also acknowledges their necessity: "people do have to work with others . . . it *is* an age of organization" (p. 13). But, he adds, we already know this all too well. What is needed is a "counteremphasis" on "individualism *within* organization life" (p. 12); the individual must recognize the power that organization has over him and "assert himself against it" (p. 14):

> The fault is not in organization, in short, it is in our worship of it. It is in our vain quest for a utopian equilibrium, which would be horrible if it ever did come to pass; it is in the soft-minded denial that there is a conflict between the individual and society. (p. 14)

This is as clear a statement as one can find of the moralizers' position: there has been a loss of the old values (individualism is more accurate than Protestant Ethic, says Whyte) on the part of the individual, the individual is in conflict with society, and the individual must assert himself (but within existing structures).

After describing the individual at work in the large organization, Whyte follows him home to suburbia. Here he finds togethereness with a vengeance, the group-pressures of the conference room and office reflected throughout in friendship circles and voluntary associations, church, school, and *Kaffeeklatsch*. He stresses again the effacement of individual differences in the "quest for normalcy," the "spurious ideal of middle-class adjustment" (pp. 440-441). Here means have not only undermined ends; they have obliterated them completely. Whyte asks, adjustment to what? It is sterile, he says, to teach adjustment and well-roundedness, to learn the techniques before the content of getting along without knowing why and to what end. Riesman, of course, had emphasized this as a salient characteristic of other-direction: "Approval itself, irrespective of content, becomes almost the only unequivocal good in this situation: one makes good when one is approved of" (1950, p. 49).

What Whyte had to say about the organization man, Riesman and his collaborators (1950) had already said about the other-directed man—the type described as emerging in the upper-middle class of our larger cities. Like Whyte, but on a broader canvas, Riesman pointed out structural changes that had outmoded the Protestant ethic (inner-direction). As society became highly industrialized and urbanized and its economy mature, problems of production, technology, and financing became routinized. That is to say, what had previously depended on the innovation of individuals became institutionalized, or "built-into" society:

. . . on the whole, contemporary society, especially America, no longer requires and rewards the old enterprise and the old zeal. . . . The invention and adoption of new improvements can be routinized, built into the system, so to speak, rather than into the men who run the system. (Riesman, 1954, p. 104)

With these changes in society and in the demands made on individuals, the other-directed man turns from production to consumption, "from craft skill to manipulative skill," from the hardness of material to the "softness" of men (1950, pp. 131-47). Thus Riesman also takes structural changes into account; however, he not only accepts them in general as a necessary consequence of industrialization but also scans them thoughtfully to see what advantages they may offer. While he, too, is concerned with the "individual" side of the equation, his emphasis is not so much a plea for the reassertion of old values (they had their shortcomings, too) as for the exploration of new areas of choice that would open up avenues to what he has called autonomy—a term I believe he prefers to individualism in this context. He defines autonomy as a self-awareness that enables the individual to conform to society but leaves him free to choose whether to conform or not.

In this way, Riesman tries to avoid judging the shift from inner- to other-direction because he sees limitations in both, although his delineation of the latter tends to put it in an unfavorable light, as he candidly admits. He speaks of the "nerve of failure"—"the courage to face aloneness and the possibility of defeat in one's personal life or one's work without being morally destroyed" (1954, p. 55). To reverse, in this way, the failure of nerve, is clearly an individual responsibility—an act of autonomy.

We have then, on the one hand, the assertion that the individual's basic value-commitments have changed—from passion for freedom to desire for security, from Protestant ethic to social ethic, from the goals of inner-direction to the approval-seeking of other-direction. Moreover, we have the generally prevalent judgment that this change is bad.

On the other hand, we have the analyses of what has happened to bring about this state of affairs—at the cultural level, the preoccupation with scientific and technological means and the depreciation of humanistic ends; at the social level, the routinization of economic production and the consequent expropriation of individual initiative; and within the society, the development of complex organization with its pressures for individual submission to the group. But I agree with Rieff when he says, "To Whyte, as to Riesman, the future of American culture revolves mainly around the question of rehabilitating the individual" (1957, p. 306).

The empirical evidence alleging changes in value-commitments is considerably harder to adduce than that on the cultural and social changes just listed; nor can the former be (although it often is) simply derived from the latter. In addition to the evidence put forward by Riesman, Whyte, and others not considered here, probably the most thorough presentation of evidence on values and on commitment to them in contemporary American society is to be found in Clyde Kluckhohn's "Have There Been Discernible Shifts in American Values During the Past Generation?" (1958).

Kluckhohn's answer, after interpreting a massive amount of evidence, is yes. Avoiding any judgment as to the (un)desirability of the change he discerns, he sums up by saying that American values, stable over a period of a hundred and fifty years, may have been undergoing certain shifts in emphasis over the past generation. (If one assumes that values are the causal factor, then one explains the current, altered situation as *either* a loss of commitment to old values *or* a change in the values themselves.) These value shifts are, paraphrased, as follows:

1. A shift from strictly personal to group values and an increase in "conservatism."
   The machine is coming to be taken as a model for human behavior.
2. A rise in "psychological values"—mental health, child-rearing, etc. But the goal is "less the achievement of uniqueness and more the achievement of similarity."
3. A shift from "future success" to "respectable and stable security" seen in shorter time range.
4. A rise in esthetic values.
5. A rise in value of institutionalized religion, but from need for group affiliation and stability rather than from intensified personal religious life.
6. "Heterogeneity" (meaning tolerance of differences and diversity) is becoming the organizing principle of the American value system.
7. The ideal for American woman and her place in society has altered as have our sexual codes.
8. An increase in overt concern for abstract standards; greater emphasis on explicit values. (1958, p. 204)

Writing as a social scientist and not as a critic of American society, Kluckhohn's conclusions are considerably more cautious than most of those stated in the periodicals I have been reading; yet some of his interpretations of the evidence support many of the *empirical* (although not necessarily the evaluative) assertions made by the moralizers. Although the emotional tone of the language may be different, items 1,

2, 3, 5, and 7 are in general agreement with them. While Kluckhohn pointedly considers the "conformity" issue a red herring (I shall refer to his comments later), he does seem to agree that there has been a decline in the Protestant Ethic (1958, p. 192).

His evidence in support of item 6 seems to be in direct contradiction to the ideological assumption that social pressures and forces are effacing differences—individual or otherwise. The same evidence, however, has been used by the advocates of the mass-culture theory to support the notion that tolerance of diversity leads to its absorption in an undifferentiated whole, or mass. In other words, distinctions are often maintained, it is said, by conflict; bland toleration of them only results in a dissolving of boundaries. Their position might be stated in this way: toleration of heterogeneity leads to homogenization.

Kluckhohn's support for his conclusion in item 8 runs along the following lines:

> Among those who have rejected the Puritan Ethic or who are, at most, apathetic toward its tenets, there is often an extremely active search for explicit values that educated men who accept mass organizations as the normal centers of their lives can believe in and live by. (1958, p. 198)

As is the case in item 6, intellectuals have used the same evidence to put their case somewhat more strongly—that is, that the weakening of old values has led to a search for security in the return to religion, or a search for purpose in the "religion of the organization" (frequently portrayed in novels about high-pressure, overdedicated executives).

The Hedonism of Consumption.—Kluckhohn's conclusion in item 4—a rise in esthetic values—was drawn from evidence he presented in the body of his text under the rubric "hedonistic, present-time orientation" (1958, p. 192). He was mainly concerned with the increase of recreational activities in the society and the concomitant implication of an increase in "taking pleasure now" at the possible expense of "working for the future." Kluckhohn states that he does not "employ hedonism in the pejorative sense" but is rather referring to leisure—esthetic and expressive activities. He also adds: "And I would say that there is abundant evidence that popular taste in the United States is improving."

Others are less sanguine. In the first place, they would not support the assertion that standards of taste are improving; for the prevailing standards are said to be not those of esthetic quality but insignia of status, or credentials of acceptability in the group.

Moreover, most intellectuals would not limit, as Kluckhohn did, the phenomenon of hedonism to the esthetic aspects of recreation; they would extend it to include what is seen as an excessive acquiring of consumers' goods. This alleged preoccupation with consumption is looked at not as an epiphenomenon of market conditions and the like but rather as a failure on the part of individuals to live up to the proper values. Individuals have "gone soft," so to speak. It is seen as one more evidence of the decline of the Protestant Ethic, a desertion of the principles of thrift, of planning for the future, of earning what one has. The imputation of extravagant consumption also dovetails neatly with that of the degrading effects of technology, since a large share of consumer expenditures goes into "gadgets."

Philip Rieff similarly emphasizes this point of view by imputing a religious aspect to this alleged attitude toward consumption:

False consciousness is here to stay; it is the happy psychic condition of a mature and still dynamic industrial civilization that has worked back through a religion of transcendence [as in the Protestant Ethic] to a religion of immanence based on a supra-primitive fetishism of infinitely variable commodities. (1956, p. 369)

Krutch, deploring the current preoccupation with consumption, states that the old value of savings has been inverted to "have fun now and pay later." "Scorn not the common man, for he will eat baby food, and later smoke and drink and learn to understand psychological obsolescence" (1956, p. 469). The ideological position on this issue can be summed up as follows: the increased emphasis on consumption signifies an increased evaluation of gratifying present, and often quite unnecessary, wants; it devalues the importance of hard work and of depriving oneself of present pleasures for the sake of building for the future. As Russell Lynes waggishly put it, "we keep our noses to the rhinestones." Dwight Macdonald has even suggested that our national motto should be "I got mine and screw you, Jack!" (1958a, p. 315).

Conclusion.—In the relationship between the individual and society, conceived of in terms of excessive conformity and regulation, the moralizing ideology focusses on the individual side of the relationship. Whatever structural conditions it sees as contributing to this undesirable state of affairs, the *individual is responsible* for resisting them; his resistance—with that of millions of others—will bring structural conditions into line. Our salvation lies "in the hearts and minds of men." Moralizing ideology expresses the hope, as Niebuhr put it, that human "reason" will be so purified that all social institutions will gradually become the bearers of a universal human will. The institutions, the real factors, will become the natural epiphenomena of human "will" and "reason," the ideal factors. The principal cause of excessive conformity and regulation is the individual's desertion of values; the cure, his reassertion of them.

To return to our metaphor of a "runaway inflation," the moralizers see the problem as one wherein the individual is all too eager to buy any "goods" that are offered on the "market"—be they literally consumers' goods, or figuratively peer-group approval and the security of togetherness. The low quality of popular demand has allowed standards to deteriorate. The price of the goods offered is too high and will soon bankrupt the individual of his human capital—his uniqueness, the qualities that differentiate him from everybody else. The inflation is to be cured on the buyers' side by arresting overspending; the cheap currency of conformity, which fluctuates with transient tastes, must be restored to a sound basis—the gold standard of lasting values.

4

The Reformers' Approach

In the case of reforming ideology, the same issue—the assertion of individual autonomy—as that concerning the moralizers is at stake, but it is looked at from the other side of the relationship. The individual is not only unable to resist structural conditions, he is so shaped by them that his position in society determines his entire outlook on life —his attitudes toward others as well as toward himself. The real factors determine the ideal factors. This social conditioning is said to deprive him even of the leverage within himself by which he could judge the conditions objectively. This formulation is summed up in Fromm's concept of the socially patterned defect, which is said to exist when a majority of members of a society share the inability, because of widespread social conditions, to attain freedom, spontaneity, a genuine expression of self. They think they are adjusted because they know of no other alternatives (Fromm, 1954).

The individual's ability *apart* from these conditions to attain this freedom and spontaneity is not seen as problematical; that is, it is assumed to be "given." Human nature, says Fromm, has an intrinsic quality of its own, independent of what society and culture do with it. The underlying assumption is that man is essentially good if he is just given the right conditions; he is evil only under adverse conditions. Fromm considers Freud's theory about man as dualistic, as seeing man driven by two contradictory forces; he qualifies the Freudian position by saying that

[37]

the destructiveness Freud thought inherent in all human beings is a result of *frustrating conditions*. In an illuminating illustration, he likens man's potentialities to the seed from which a tree grows:

> To say that something exists "potentially" means not only that it will exist in the future but that this future existence is already prepared in the present. This relationship between the present and the future stage of development can be described by saying that the future virtually exists in the present. Does this mean that the future stage will necessarily come into being if the present stage exists? Obviously not. If we say that the tree is potentially present in the seed, it does not mean that a tree *must* develop from every seed. The actualization of a potentiality depends on the presence of certain conditions which are, in the case of the seed, for instance, proper soil, water, and sunlight. (1947, p. 217)

He goes on to say that if conditions are unfavorable, the seed will not develop into a tree but will rot, dry up, or become deformed. Fromm does not go so far as to say that destructiveness is not inherent at all in human beings; he assigns to it the quality of a "secondary potentiality" that is "actualized if the proper [i.e., unfavorable] conditions are present" (1954, p. 218). In the end, his position comes to this:

> We have shown that man is not necessarily evil but becomes evil only if the proper conditions for his growth and development are lacking. The evil has no independent existence of its own, it is the absence of the good, the result of the failure to realize life. (1954, p. 218)

If we move to a more macroscopic level, we can see a similar point of view among *one wing* of those concerned about mass culture (a fuller discussion of this topic will be presented later, in Chapter 5), or mass society in general. The problem, this point of view holds, is not in the so-called "masses" themselves, but in their being molded and corrupted ("massified" is the customary expression) by social conditions. Says Eugene Walter:

> In a society that tragically dehumanizes personality, sensitive observers must respond in some fashion to the evidence of cultural depression

around them. . . . Actually, disorder is *not an inherent attribute* [my italics] of the mass but a condition within it. (1956, p. 78)

Marcuse takes an even more radical position. Basing his approach on his interpretation of Freud's later metapsychological works, Marcuse states that civilization itself is repressive: ". . . even the highest values of civilization, in so far as they contain inhibited and aim-diverted sexuality, inevitably pre-suppose and perpetuate un-freedom and suppression" (Marcuse and Fromm, 1956, p. 79). Although Marcuse and Fromm do not agree at all with each other's formulation of the issue, it seems to me that they share the basic assumption that man has an inherent (and inherently unproblematical) nature, and that external conditions, however conceived, frustrate its growth. The crux of the problem, says Marcuse, is the repressive control over man's *nature*. Man, instead of becoming an individual, becomes a social atom because of "surplus-repression," the collective repression of social domination (1955a, pp. 35, 97).

What conditions do the reformers see as "social sources of evil," or socially patterned defects? They cover a somewhat extensive range: the economic aspects of production and consumption; the political features of bureaucracy, industrialism, and capitalism; and the allegedly baleful influence of mass culture. Different spokesmen emphasize different aspects; but nearly all are in agreement about the relation of these conditions to the individual, and their understanding of this relation centers around the concepts of alienation and loss of identity. We will turn first to the conditions themselves.

Consumption.—Where the moralizers look on the current preoccupation with consumers' goods as a hedonistic "going-soft," the reformers see the individual victimized. In the first place, a high level of consumption is forced on the buying public in order to sop up the outpouring of an overproductive economy. If the public does not continue to buy, the Keynesian consequences of increasing inventories and subsequent unemployment will be all too familiar. Thrift and savings,

Puritan standards to the contrary, are the last things we can afford. The market is kept moving with built-in obsolescence, instalment-buying, and the persuasion of advertising.

In part, this is seen as a consequence of an overemphasis on productivity for productivity's sake. Galbraith traces this overemphasis to the inadequacies of an economic theory that was rooted in the poverty and scarcity of the past and did not foresee the present state of affluence (1958, p. 5). From a vastly different frame of reference, Marcuse arrives at the same conclusion: productivity, he says, is "one of the most strictly protected values of modern culture," but with the development of a mature society, the basis of scarcity has been undermined and productivity has tended to become an end in itself (1955a, pp. 155-56). Marcuse, however, reaches beyond Galbraith in explaining underlying causes; it is not merely the ideologically time-bound limitations of economic theory that account for this phenomenon, but the fact that —once set free—the rationale of productivity gains an autonomy and justification of its own instead of serving individual needs. As in the moralizers' view of science and technology, there has been a reversal of the means-end relationship.

Melvin Seiden puts it: "Is it an exaggeration to claim that economic means and ends have been reversed in America and that to a remarkable extent we consume, irrationally, for the sake of production?" (1958, p. 277). He concedes that abundance and indulgence are probably preferable to scarcity and austerity, but we are not familiar with the new evils that result from the reversal of the usual condition. Others, however, seem more certain than Seiden of what the evils are. Like the moralizers, they see excessive consumption as corrupting, but they differ in regarding the corruption as due not to individual weakness but to social pressures, if not to implicit social conspiracy. Thus, the impotence engendered by hedonism may even aid and abet political apathy:

Democracy may need daily practice to maintain the personality structure it requires. . . . In his present powerless, dependent position, and *lulled by abundance* [my italics], what stimulus has the individual to participate in or care about the political affairs of the nation? (Reagan, 1956, p. 351)

Worse yet, undesirable though this abundance may or may not be, the individual is said to have little autonomous choice in determining his wants or needs; that is, there is *practically no consumer sovereignty.* Consumer decisions, says Galbraith, are not independent wants democratically arrived at, but are synthesized, that is, contrived, by advertising and emulation. Advertising is particularly regarded as a malignant force; admen, says Vance Packard (1957), are: 1) masters of economic destiny; 2) engineers of political campaigns; 3) patrons of social science; 4) dictators of entertainment; 5) tastemakers; and 6) merchants of discontent.

It is in this last imputed role that admen are able to take advantage of emulation. Emulation is no longer a simple matter—as it was in simpler days—of keeping up with, or ahead of, the Joneses. Now it is a complicated matter of winning approval by having the "right" consumption preferences, as Riesman has pointed out (1950, pp. 78-82)— complicated because the standards for those preferences are constantly shifting and the distinctions between the standards of different groups of people are often very subtle and at best only marginally differentiated.

Finally, the price paid for this questionable affluence is too high. Not only does the consumer have to pay for all these things he does not "really" need, but he sacrifices his leisure in using them. Says Marcuse:

The high standard of living in the domain of the great corporations is *restrictive* in a concrete sociological sense: the goods and services that the individuals buy control their needs and petrify their faculties. In exchange for the commodities that enrich their life, the individuals sell not only their labor but also their free time. The better living is offset by the all-pervasive control over living. (1955b, p. 100)

Power and Authority.

In pre-capitalist societies, power was known and personal. The individual could see who was powerful, and he could understand the means of his power. His responses of obedience and fear were explicit and concrete; and if he was in revolt, the targets of that revolt were also explicit and concrete. Comments H. D. Lasswell, "Once your eye lights on the Indian who lies in wait behind a tree, you know you are being ambushed. But you may see a modern financier at his desk for hours a day for years and catch no clue to the nature of the security structure which he has set up to ambush investors." . . . In an impersonalized and more anonymous system of control, explicit responses are not so possible: anxiety is likely to replace fear; insecurity to replace worry. The problem is who really has power, for often the tangled and hidden system seems a complex, yet organized irresponsibility. When power is delegated from a distant center, the one immediately over the individual is not so different than the individual himself; he does not decide either; he too is a part of the network by means of which individuals are controlled. . . . And so insecurity and striving are not attached to political symbols, but are drained off by the distractions of amusement, the frenzied search for commodities, or turned in upon the self as busy little frustrations. . . . On the one hand politics is bureaucratized, and on the other, there is a mass indifference. (Mills, 1951, pp. 349-350)

We have seen that Whyte looked on large-scale organization as a necessary condition—if not necessary evil—of modern society to be resisted by the individual. The reformers, however, see it as a sufficient condition *per se* of social evil that no one *can* resist. As Mills has put it, how can anyone resist an "anonymous system"? Nor do reformers see this phenomenon as limited to the context of organization, for the social patterns and psychological attitudes it engenders are said to permeate the entire system. Michael Reagan spells out for us how this state of affairs comes about. "Bigness," he says, has taken over. With the increasing dominance of large-scale organization, more and more people work under conditions where they carry out orders handed down to them. He then asks:

Is it not possible that even the desire, let alone the ability, to share in political decision making may atrophy through the continued impact of simply receiving decisions made from above in one's economic activities? . . . Whether the dependent, paternalistic, authoritarian life of modern economic institutions is compatible with independent, self-reliant, democratic political institutions may still be an open question, but it is surely a question. (1956, p. 350)

To Fromm, the answer is all too clear. Going considerably farther than Reagan, he sees the "authority-structure" as having an impact well beyond just political institutions. Like Mills, he contrasts the past, when one at least knew who exploiter and exploited were, with the present:

> . . . instead of rational and irrational but *overt* authority, we find *anonymous* authority—the authority of public opinion and the market: instead of the individual conscience, the need to adjust and be approved of: instead of the sense of pride and mastery, an ever-increasing though mainly unconscious sense of powerlessness. (Fromm, 1955b, p. 99)
>
> The mechanism through which the anonymous authority operates is *conformity.* (p. 153)

Thus, Fromm does not limit the notion of authority to a specified relationship when one in a superordinate status holds power over another in a subordinate status; he generalizes it to include all sanctioning "powers" whatever—e.g., opinion and approval. Furthermore, such sanctions—rewards as well as punishments—are seen as limitations on individual freedom, restricting the range of free choices. If authority is conceived of as being invoked wherever sanctions are imposed, then the implication seems to be that practically all social relationships are at least essentially, if not completely, political in nature.

Harvey Wheeler makes this implication explicit:

> . . . growing segments of the population have suffered bureaucratic enfeudation. It is this condition that is increasingly bemoaned in literature on the helplessness of the lonely crowd, the bleakness of living conditions for the "mass man" and the "organization man." (1957, p. 309)

The middle class suffers, Wheeler says, because it is forced to consume standardized commodities, and wives have to go to work to help pay for them. And then they too become part of the bureaucratic organization. "Bureaucratic man is not able to control by his own individual effort anything necessary to his life, liberty, or pursuit of happiness" (p. 303). He has to buy from bureaucratic chain stores, live in mass suburbs, and work for huge firms. Therefore:

. . . in a bureaucratic culture sources of desequilibrium [sic] previously economic are converted into political forms. (p. 302)

*Implicit in the conditions of life in a bureaucratic culture is the
conversion of all problems into political problems.* (p. 306)

In short, modern man is increasingly dependent and powerless. As society becomes more highly organized on a grand
scale, the range of individual freedom of choice, of control,
declines. In addition to the necessities of hierarchical and
anonymous authority, there are also those of co-ordinating
an increasingly complex system. The mechanical regularity
of the assembly line that Chaplin satirized applies as well
to the commuter tied to his train schedule. Thus Harvey
Swados, in reviewing Spectorsky's *The Exurbanites*, suggests
that the stigmata that formerly characterized only the proletariat are now being transferred to the swelling millions
of suburbanites:

Are we actually becoming a nation of tense, anxious and wretched
white-collar proletarians, with nothing to lose but our uninsured
TV antennae? (1956, p. 206)

Alienation.—At the beginning of this section, I suggested
that the central concern of the intellectual ideology was the
individual's freedom to choose for and to become himself.
The mounting condemnation of modern industrial society
referred to in these last pages clearly regards this freedom as
severely curtailed at many points. It appears that the very
instrumentalities of society have become ends in themselves,
obeying their own laws, and, in consequence, progressively
limiting the range of choices open to modern man.

The economies of mass production are said to limit the
variety of goods available to him. The huge productive ap-
paratus—created to lay at his feet an affluence hitherto un-
dreamed of—has unleashed a frivolous prodigality that he
must struggle to support. The complexity of organization
increases his dependence as bureaucracy—in accordance with
"Parkinson's law"—becomes self-proliferating. As Actaeon was
made the prey of his own hounds for his presumption, so man
has fallen into unwitting bondage to his own instrumentali-

ties. Whatever problems atomic power poses in and of itself, it is also the symbol *par excellence* of this predicament.

Max Weber has described the way in which this "instrumentalization" has come about as the process of *rationalization*. He defines rationalization as both "an increasing theoretical mastery of reality by means of increasingly precise and abstract concepts" and "the methodical attainment of a definitely given and practical end by means of an increasingly precise calculation of adequate means" (1946, p. 293). Weber points out that these two components are very different although they belong inseparably together. In relation to the ideological issues discussed here, it is the second type that we are concerned with, for it is the methodical calculation of means—in whatever context—that has profoundly altered patterns of human behavior and has, as the intellectuals would maintain, included man among the means to be calculated. With important qualifications (that I shall make later) as to just what aspects of man's activity this includes, this proposition is unquestionably valid. Marx, for example, quite rightly pointed out that economic production was not simply a matter of "non-social" technology, but that the relationship to the means of production was itself a *social* relationship (although his conclusion about its nature is another problem).

The process of rationalization, then, has given *carte blanche* to the division of labor as the most effective means of attaining given ends. With the division of labor, man can no longer hunt in the morning, fish in the afternoon, and criticize after dinner—as Marx puts it—but must *specialize* in being a hunter, *or* a fisherman, *or* a critical critic. He has no other choice. The consequence of this restriction is *alienation*.

In the ideological context the concept of alienation has as its frame of reference man's relation to self, to nature, to society, or to God. And alienation is meant to be understood as an undesirable state of affairs. As F. H. Heinemann puts it: "a preceding unity and harmony has been transformed into disunity and disharmony" (1958, p. 9). He says that Hegel was the first to treat the problem of alienation—in this sense —seriously, dealing with the alienation of mind from the products of its own creation. (Hegel used the terms *Entfremdung*—estrangement, and *Entäusserung*—externalization, or parting with.) Marx took over the conception of alienation from Hegel, but transformed it (by standing Hegel on his head, as we all know) to refer to the alienation of labor, and —ultimately—of man himself. It is, of course, Marx's usage that is the source of current ideological reference.

David Braybrooke summarizes Marx's concept of alienation as follows:

In capitalistic society the typical situation of the worker is one in which he must perform tiresome labor on objects that he will not himself use or own. They will instead be claimed by his employer when they are finished, and he in turn will attempt to sell them in the market, without prescribing, any more than the worker prescribes, anything regarding their ultimate destination and use. From the worker's point of view (and to a degree, though a lesser degree, the employer's as well), the objects so manufactured are produced without a purpose; the only reason the worker does the work at all is to acquire enough in wages to buy outside the factory the necessities of life. Thus the worker is alienated from the objects he produces, since they are appropriated by others and used for other people's purposes, not his own; and from his work, since he has no genuine personal interest in it. He is also alienated from his fellowmen: from his employer and other capitalists, because they have privileges that he is denied; from other workers, because he must compete with them for jobs; from both these groups, because he is prevented, under the conditions of the market, from joining with them in expressing a social purpose in production, by bringing it all under a general plan, which the members of society would collaborate in developing and carrying out. (1958, p. 326)

Through the division of labor, the worker ultimately becomes alienated from himself, because he becomes a commodity that he must sell on the labor market.

In addition to this economic aspect of alienation, there is the political one as well, and here the problem of alienation of property comes into the picture. The man who owns and works his own property has power over his own work; he can manage himself and plan his working day. But the man who does not own property must work for someone else who does, and must submit to his authority. "The owner," as Mills puts it, "manages the working life of the non-owner" (1951, p. 14).

As we have seen, the reformers regard what Marx had to say about the factory worker as equally applicable to the white collar worker in the bureaucracy, and—by extending the same line of reasoning—to society in general where the individual's freedom to make choices and control his own life is asserted to be constricted by increasing routinization and dependence. Thus, not only man's labor but man himself becomes a commodity that he must "offer on the market" in order to be "accepted by the group." The principles of the economic market are in this way extrapolated to what Fromm calls the "interpersonal market"; the individual must offer a personality that will "sell" in terms of current demand.

Others, as well as Fromm, interpret the current state of affairs as an extension, in one way or another, of economic principles. Says Heinemann:

Alienation is a fact. There exists a feeling of estrangement in modern man which has considerably increased during the last hundred years. It is connected with certain changes in human society, with the agglomeration of millions of people in great cities cut off from Nature, with the Industrial Revolution, and with the collectivizing trend bound up with machine production. (1958, p. 9)

Anticipating the same theme that Hannah Arendt later developed at length in *The Human Condition*, Henri Rabasseire (1956b) points out the difference between *work*—the creative product of *homo faber*—and *labor*—the repetitive expenditure of human energy by what Arendt calls *animal laborans*. Productivity, says Rabasseire, has enthroned efficiency (an economic principle) in place of the old qualities of workmanship. "The satisfaction is not in creating the product [work]; it is in productivity [labor]. The worker is completely estranged from his product . . ." (1956b, p. 40). Taking a longer perspective and embracing art as well, Clement Greenberg says that in the archaic past, work and art were fused, but "five thousand years of urban history have gradually separated these activities with their implicit ends and sealed them off from each other" (1953b, p. 61).

Heinemann sums up this point of view succintly in terms of the concept of alienation by saying that Marx's materialistic alienation has led to "institutional alienation":

Human institutions—the state, the government, the civil service, the party, the factory—have become impersonal and anonymous [cf. Mills and Fromm] powers of enormous strength which the individual tries in vain to master. Thence arises the growing sense of frustration, anxiety and despair, which pervades the Western hemisphere. (1958, p. 168)

The prophets of woe, like the American R. Seidenberg, tell us that this trend must lead in any society, whether democratic, fascist or socialist, inexorably to a condition of total crystallization in its structural edifice [as in 1984] and to a final depersonalization of man. (p. 9)

Perhaps the phrase that best describes this human plight is *purposelessness in life*. And this purposelessness has come about because means have become dissociated, or alienated, from ends and, in the process, have displaced them. Whether the process be attributed to the division of labor or technology, to efficiency or organization, it is what Weber meant by rationalization—calculating the effectiveness of means independently of their given ends. But, according to the testimony here presented, the "givenness" of ends has become unhinged along the way.

Thus, we come full circle back to the humanists' lament about the means-end relationship, although we have arrived at it by a different line of analysis. The humanists, it seems to me, arrived at the same conclusion with reference to Weber's first definition of rationalization, "the increasing theoretical mastery of reality by means of increasingly precise and abstract concepts."

Conclusion.—According to the reformers, the alleged subversion of ends is located in social conditions. Man's essential goodness and the individual's innate capacity to choose for himself are taken for granted. Failure to utilize the ability to choose is attributed to the social environment. If favorable conditions were present, the requisite value-commitments of the individual would be automatically generated. The *ideal factors* (values, etc.) are the epiphenomena of the *real* factors (the social conditions that determine the distribution of power). These ideologists hope, in Niebuhr's words, to create "perfect men by eliminating the social sources of evil."

In terms of our metaphor of a "runaway inflation," the reformers see the problem as one in which the individual is pressured by the excessive regulation of "society"; if we apply the language of the economic case (as do many of these ideologists), it would be to say that individual has no consumer sovereignty.

5

Psychological and Cultural Aspects: Loss of Identity and Mass Culture

Loss of Identity:
The Psychological Counterpart

The "purposelessness" in modern life—seen as a "breakdown of values" on one side and as alienation on the other —has led many, especially those with psychoanalytic training or interests, to be concerned about its impact on the individual's personality.

The Moralizers' Approach.—The "breakdown of values" is interpreted in different ways: as a loss of religious faith— or, in Tillich's phrase, a loss of ultimate concern; as an undermining of humanistic eternal verities; or—in Riesman's and Whyte's more specific reference—as an obsolescence of the old inner-directed goals and a decline of the Protestant Ethic. Beyond these differences, however, is the common notion that whatever once gave meaningful purpose to life has deteriorated; normative order has given way to a random indeterminacy.

Under such circumstances, how can the individual know where he is going in life? Without the purpose that makes sense out of life, how can he make sense out of himself? Instead, he suffers a *loss of identity*. As Allen Wheelis, a San Franciscan psychoanalyst puts it, "Values determine goals, and goals determine identity" (1958, p. 174). Erik Erikson, whose *Childhood and Society* is a distinguished contribution to this problem, defines identity as "the ability to experience one's self as something that has continuity and sameness, and to act accordingly" (1950, p. 38). With values purportedly collapsing, or at least in a state of flux, this continuity and sameness are severely threatened. With life-goals indeterminate, identity is indeterminate: "To escape the danger of a conviction [being convicted] for being different from the 'others' requires that one can be different—in look and talk and manner—from *oneself* as one was yesterday" (Riesman, 1950, p. 95).

Both Wheelis and Erikson present clinical evidence to support the increasing salience of this problem. Wheelis suggests that patients' mental disturbances are generally of a different order than those of the past; hysteria resulting from repression has tended to be replaced by character disorders. Where formerly patients had strong superegos, whose punitiveness brought them to the analyst's couch, and a definite sense of identity, today the superego (the psychological agency for values) and the sense of identity have declined. The patient expects the analyst to hand him an identity, to answer his question of "Who am I?"

Similarly, Erikson:

. . . the patient of today suffers most under the problem of what he should believe in and who he should—or, indeed, might—be or become, while the patient of early psychoanalysis suffered most under inhibitions which prevented him from being what and who he thought he knew he was. (1950, p. 239)

The study of identity, then, becomes as strategic in our time as the study of sexuality was in Freud's time. (p. 242)

The Reformers' Approach.—The reformers view the loss of identity in terms of alienation. They see it as a consequence of the loosening and disintegration of structural ties; for the sense of identity comes from being meaningfully related to others in an organic community. In such a community, the individual stands in definite relations to these others. His identity arises from knowing what to expect of them and they of him. The very determinacy of these relations makes it possible, it is said, for him to acquire his identity in terms of appropriate models whose patterns of behavior are not obscured by the complexities of "abstraction" and anonymous authority. A boy can learn how to become a man through the manifest example of his father, as Ruth Benedict has pointed out (1955).

In the alienated society, these continuities break down. The progressive alienation of labor, property, personal relationships, and the like, leads to the alienation of self, which is the same thing as loss of identity. In addition, the reformers assert, community ties are disrupted as a result of the constant moving around that Americans do. Suburban life epitomizes this transience and its effects. According to Newman:

> . . . the American suburb is the institutionalization of mobility. . . . In the desert of the suburb, community life has lost whatever vestiges of meaning it ever had for Americans; if any community life exists at all, it is frantically on the synthetic level of suburban club and church; it has a tinny quality betraying a lack of conviction on the part of all concerned. (1957, pp. 256-7)

Mass Culture

The intellectuals' concern with what they consider the leveling of distinctions in American society is particularly acute with regard to mass culture—the cultural content mass-produced by mass media for mass audiences. In ideological discourse, they usually distinguish mass culture from two other types: high and folk. Thus Macdonald writes:

> For about a century, Western culture has really been two cultures: the traditional kind—let us call it "High Culture"—that is chronicled in the textbooks, and a "Mass Culture" manufactured wholesale for the market. . . . It is sometimes called "Popular Culture," but I think "Mass Culture" a more accurate term since its distinctive mark is that it is solely and directly an article for mass consumption, like chewing gum. A work of High Culture is occasionally popular, after all, though this is increasingly rare. (1957, p. 59)

Despite Macdonald's ease of definition, the distinction between high and mass culture is not easily made explicit, however much "everyone knows" what it is. In the above quotation, Macdonald defines high culture as the "traditional kind"; in this case, the criterion—as far as it is implied —seems to be solely the test of time. Approval is placed on that which is retained and "chronicled." The criterion he uses to define mass culture is of a different order; since the test of time cannot be applied, he uses the intent of the producer of culture with regard to the size of audience he had in mind when he created—or "manufactured"—his product. The proposition seems to be that any product intentionally marketed for a large audience is *ipso facto* not up to the standards of high culture.

Obviously—and perhaps fortunately—there are difficulties in laying down standards that one can apply to any cultural product and then pronounce it high or mass, independently of the intended audience or without waiting for time to pass. The faddisms of high culture bear eloquent testimony to this problem, even with respect to works of the past, as the guardians of the best-that-has-been-thought-and-said debate about whether Browning, or even Milton, is "in" or "out." Suffice it to say, there is no problem in drawing the line between Shakespeare (unadulterated by television, of course) and Mickey Spillane, with an indeterminate boundary somewhere in between.

In addition to these two levels, Macdonald defines a third: folk culture—the "spontaneous, autochthonous expression of the people, shaped by themselves, pretty much without the benefit of High Culture, to suit their own needs" (1957, p. 60).

The central proposition in mass-culture theory is that mass culture corrupts the standards of excellence in high culture and at the same time effaces the unique quality of folk culture. It is, in short, one more agency of homogenization in modern society:

Never before have the sacred and the profane, the genuine and the specious, the exalted and debased, been so thoroughly mixed that they are all but indistinguishable. *Who can sort one from the other* [my italics] when they are built into a single slushy compost? (Bernard Rosenberg, 1957, p. 5)

Mass culture is said to bring this state of affairs about in two ways. First, it "mines high culture" for ideas, as Macdonald puts it. It uses the content of high culture as its raw material and then debases it so that it will be acceptable (can be sold) to a large audience (the masses). Says Louis Kronenberger, ". . . everything is tampered with or touched up, or adulterated and watered down . . . in an effort to make it pay" (1951-52, pp. 19-20). Content is abridged or lengthened, the scene or the medium is changed; in the process all is vulgarized (Kronenberger, 1953). In an effort to capture the largest possible audience, the lowest common denominator of taste is appealed to. Because such an audience does not possess adequate criteria of judgment, the expected reactions are built in; that is, the audience is presented with simplified content and is told as well what to think about it. This standardization inhibits idiosyncrasy and destroys the sense of continuity with the past (Greenberg, 1953a).

Second, the reformers assert that mass culture also undermines folk culture, which—before the days of mass media and mobility—was insulated from homogenization on its natural site, be it countryside, village, or ghetto. Now mass culture borrows from folk culture as well as from high, as in jazz and folk-singing. And the urbanized ex-folk desert their "spontaneous" folk patterns for newer but more vulgar products. Whatever the effect may be on those so deprived, the intellectuals view the result as an additional loss of cultural diversity: the cultural heritage is robbed of some of its idiosyncratic features. (The argument is parallel to that which claims that psychoanalysis deprives people of their individuality.)

Apparently with what Macdonald calls "folk culture" in mind, T. S. Eliot (1948) lists regional diversity as one of the three important conditions for culture. He finds such diversity enriching and points out that British culture, for example, would suffer without the survival of "satellite cultures" such as the Welsh. He stresses the importance of preserving the "particularity of constituent parts" (1948, p. 62). Similarly, the American intellectual, travelling through Europe, is charmed by the diversity that Eliot praises and that Sapir found so dismally lacking in America. In Europe, each region has—it is said—its own cuisine and wines, its own distinctive style of dress, of manner and speech. In America, there is little variation, with the exception of such rapidly shrinking pockets as the deeper South or the Kentucky mountains.

Whereas folk culture in industrialized societies, especially in America, is increasingly vitiated by exposure to mass culture (even Negro shanties in the Mississippi Delta now boast TV antennae), high culture can at least take refuge in avant-gardism. In flight before the depredations of mass culture, high culture simply refuses to compete and strives for a form of expression that not only is incomprehensible to the masses but also cannot be simplified for them (Macdonald, 1957, p. 63).

The Framework for Analysis.—Although the issues in the mass-culture problem are somewhat more complex than those we have already considered, they can still be analyzed along the lines we have been following. Mass culture can be looked at as a particular application of the relationship between the individual and society with the relationship expressed as that between the masses and mass culture.

On the one hand, the intellectuals view the locus of values as residing in the masses as an aggregate of individuals whose individuality is assumed by the ideology to have been effaced; that is, the masses belong on the "value-side" of the value-social structure axis because they are seen as the repository of standards of taste and preference. Whether the masses set these standards or have them set for them depends on the ideological approach taken.

On the other hand, mass culture belongs on the social

structure-side; that is, the cultural content and the various media that transmit it are seen as conditions in the social structure that influence the setting of standards. Like the peer-group or the bureaucratic organization, mass culture is one of the *agencies of socialization*. Intellectual ideology regards this agency as having excessive and deleterious influence. It is one more source of social pressure that limits individual choice and undermines the values (in this case, the standards of what "culture" ought to be) that informed or spontaneous choice affirms.

As with the relationship between the individual and society, that between the masses and mass culture is also ideologically characterized by a "runaway inflation," where the masses are seen as all too eager to consume whatever "goods" are offered them and where the goods are sold by high-pressure techniques.

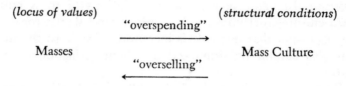

Although both the reformer and the moralist wings of the intellectual ideology agree that the value-side is being squeezed, they differ—as before—about the nature of the relationship and the underlying cause of its inflationary nature. Each approach emphasizes one component of the interchange: the value-oriented approach focuses on "overspending" and the low quality of demand wherein the masses set the standards; the structure-oriented approach focuses on "overselling" and the low quality of supply wherein the standards are set *for* the masses. There are actually two ideological schools of thought *within* the value-oriented approach itself. In addition to the view of the moralizers with which we are already familiar, there is yet another entertained by people I shall refer to as *elitists*. Both moralizers and elitists share the conclusion that the deterioration of cultural standards comes from the low quality of demand. They differ about the ways this state of affairs has come about and what should be done to remedy it. The elitist formulation is the most explicit of the two on the subject of mass culture.

Besides addressing themselves to the problems of mass culture, many elitists have analyzed the *political* nature of "mass society" as well. The literature on the latter topic is voluminous, and those who have shaped its ideas and beliefs may be broadly classified as: the elitists, who embrace an aristocratic, or conservative, approach; and others who embrace a democratic, or liberal, approach. Before proceeding with our discussion of the mass-culture problem, a brief consideration of the elitist and democratic approaches to the political nature of mass society may be helpful and should certainly reveal how closely allied that problem is to the one we are confronting. For this purpose, I turn to William Kornhauser's *The Politics of Mass Society*, where he has presented an excellent summary of these two types of interpretation. By sorting out their underlying assumptions, he has clarified the areas of selectivity in each and shown to what extent each is relevant to understanding the political features of mass society.

According to Kornhauser, the elitist, or aristocratic, interpretation holds that mass society comes about through the *loss of exclusiveness of élites* which are "composed of people who by virtue of their social position have special responsibility for standards in a given social context." In mass society, traditional authority is replaced by the rule of the masses. Jacob Burckhardt, Gustave LeBon, José Ortega y Gasset, and T. S. Eliot are among the leading exponents of this point of view.

The democratic interpretation holds that mass society comes about through the *loss of community*, or alienation. The growing atomization of industrial, urbanized society creates a widespread readiness to embrace new ties so that the population is ready prey to totalitarianism, or what Kornhauser refers to as the "domination by pseudo-community" (p. 33). Kornhauser mentions Emil Lederer and Hannah Arendt as leading representatives of this conception; I would certainly add the names of C. Wright Mills and Erich Fromm as among the more widely known.

Kornhauser contends that each of these interpretations presents only one side of the picture and that both sets of conditions are necessary in order for mass society to arise:

> Mass society is a social system in which elites are readily accessible to influence by non-elites [loss of elite exclusiveness] and non-elites are readily available for mobilization [loss of community] by elites. (1959, p. 39)

However, the elites who become accessible and those who do the mobilizing are by no means necessarily the same groups of people. Where mass culture is concerned, as we shall see, the former are the highbrow intellectual guardians of the culture and the latter are the middlebrow agents of the mass media.

The elitist and democratic interpretations, which Kornhauser has described, are respectively special cases of the value-oriented and structure-oriented types of ideological approach. Thus, the two approaches to the issue of conformity and the relationship between individual and society are ideological analyses of the "social" aspects of mass society just as the elitist and democratic interpretations are of its political aspects. The tabulation of the ideological line-up looks something like this:

	FOCUS OF ISSUE		
	"Social"	(Political)	"Cultural"
TYPE OF APPROACH			
Value-oriented		(elitists)	elitists
	moralizers		moralizers
Structure-oriented	reformers	(democratic)	reformers

We can now proceed with our analysis of the ideological approaches to the "culture" problem in the right-hand column.

The Elitists' Approach to Mass Culture.—The elitists regard mass culture, first, as the result of the *low quality of mass demand*. Traditional, or high, culture is, they believe, transmitted and preserved by an elite group qualified to be the guardians of the cultural heritage not only by superior education but by their entire style of living as well. The exclusiveness of such an elite and its authority to set and maintain standards of taste are solely responsible for the preservation of high culture. Mass culture undermines high culture when the masses arrogate this authority to themselves and unduly presume to *set their own standards*. Since the masses are less informed and less cultivated than the elite, the standards they impose are by definition inferior. Ortega y Gasset writes:

The characteristic of the hour is that the commonplace mind, knowing itself to be commonplace, has the assurance to proclaim the rights of the commonplace and to impose them wherever it will [italics omitted]. (1950, p. 12)

In this cultural context, the "rule of the masses" takes the form of a hyperdemocratic attitude toward cultural standards—"I know what I like and who is to say he knows better?" A cult of mediocrity prevails wherein claims to better taste or to excellence are suspect as snobbish. As Chiaromonte puts it, the mass man has no standards; he does not know why he thinks anything (1957, p. 176). Before the elite lost its authority, Oscar Mandel asserts, the masses looked to their betters for definition of standards: "that is why we rightly think of the masses of another day as having had better taste than mankind does today" (1958, p. 207).

How, then, according to this point of view, did this loss of elite authority come about? The first item of evidence offered is the sheer numbers of the masses. With the rapid population growth and movement to the cities that accompanied industrialization, the masses gained access, Ortega said, to complete social power. Greenberg, developing Ortega's theme, says that "by [their] sheer demographic weight and buying power, the newcomers force all levels of the cultural market down to meet the lower standards they bring with them from their culturally inferior origins (1953a, p. 565).

Second, the authority of an elite as guardians of the cultural heritage is said to have been undermined by the continual effacement of class distinctions, for the maintenance of a cultural elite depends on the stability of an aristocratic class. T. S. Eliot, among others, is a leading supporter of this proposition. Although he distinguishes between the elite, as the repository of culture, and the dominant class, all the members of which are not necessarily cultured, he does say that there is a considerable overlapping of the two. The main elite is drawn from the dominant class, which is the primary consumer of thought and art from all classes. According to him, culture must be borne by a gradation of classes, with the upper levels representing the more conscious culture. To ensure this state of affairs requires the persistence of social classes, because the family is the "primary vehicle for the transmission of culture" (1948, p. 48). Similarly, Greenberg stresses the importance of class and family; high culture, he says, is the expression of "a way of life and an ingrained sense of proportion . . . acquired during childhood, from the immediate and everyday just as much as from books and works of art" (1953a, p. 565).

A word of explanation is in order as to why the stability of class structure is not here considered as a structural condition that properly belongs to the structure-oriented wing of ideological thought. The ideological assumption of this argument is that values are seen to reside—not in individuals *per se*—but in the very class structure to which individuals are *ascribed*. Ascribed class is not a condition independent of individuals; instead, it represents them. Thus, the term "masses" is equivalent either to loss of individuality or to loss of class distinctions.

Third, the members of the cultural élite themselves are to blame for deserting their posts as cultural sentries. Their role as intellectuals is conceived to be not only as guardians of the heritage but also as critics of the society, performing what we have called the monitory function. They can best perform both roles, it is believed, by maintaining their independence of the "system," by being in the society but not of it. Free-lance thinkers have a better vantage point from which to assess what is going on than do intellectuals who have capitulated in one way or another and become part of an organization—be it foundation, university, or business —where they "spend the most alert hours of their lives being told what to do" (Mills, 1951, p. 153). When this happens, the intellectual becomes institutionalized; as an expert, says William Newman, his "brains are as useful a commodity as any other. . . . Techniques are what he spends his time on; not ideas" (1958, p. 168).

In the cultural context, Richard Chase deplores "academicism" (Macdonald's "spurious High Culture" [1957, p. 63]) and "commercialism"—in short, the "insurgence of an all encompassing middlebrowism [the mass-culture level]" (1957a, p. 129).

It should be an axiom of the cultural critic that any radical protest against conformity in this country has to begin with a declaration against middlebrowism. . . . [The] cultural health of America lies in an unremitting dialectic of extreme views and tastes . . . the middle way fails to normalize and consolidate the vitality of the extremes but destroy[s] it instead. (1957, pp. 131-132)

Instead of making this declaration, so the elitists hold, many intellectuals have abandoned their monitory role only to praise the status quo, to join in the "American celebration." Citing Galbraith as an example, Bernard Rosenberg (in a review of *American Capitalism*) says the following:

Galbraith's voice is but one in a mighty chorus of affirmationism that swells sonorously as it drowns out dissent. Intellectual agnosticism, the precondition of all scientific work, was never harder to maintain. The custodians of our culture urge us to be "positive." Pangloss has been apotheosized and his spirit, transformed into a kind of Couéism, pervades the land. . . . A good dose of corrosive criticism may turn out to be more "constructive" than everything in the yea-sayer's repertoire. (1954, p. 102)

I have included these "elitist" views under the value-oriented type of ideology because they share several underlying assumptions. First, value-commitments and the responsibility of individuals (as such, or as class members) to assert them cannot be taken for granted. Neither is the capacity to assume this responsibility innate in man nor one that will "unfold" if properly nourished by favorable conditions; rather it is seen as one that must constantly be generated by an elite.

The Ortega-Eliot line of thought and the *Dissent* writers quoted above differ about the basis of such an elite—whether it is to be ascriptively rooted in class or intellectually achieved, but both agree that cultural standards cannot be "automatically generated" but require an elite to act, so to speak, as guardians of the culture. The *Dissent* writers, in general, are structure-oriented reformers in their approach; they assume that only adverse conditions prevent the masses from forming the proper value-commitments. But they shift ground when it comes to the nature of the elite. Since intellectuals are *in* society but *not of it*, they cannot be excused by adverse conditions but must assume the responsibility for standards; hence they do not exempt from culpability those intellectuals who succumb to conditions.

Second, the value-oriented intellectuals assume that structural conditions, however undesirable, are "givens" about which little can be done. As in Whyte's advice to the organization man, it is one's duty to resist the system ("Don't watch television.").

Third, in terms of the mass-culture "market," the demand component sets the standard; that is, the masses get what they want, *and deserve*. Consumer sovereignty reigns, says van den Haag:

The elite no longer determines what is produced . . . [but] becomes the elite by producing the goods that sell, the goods that cater to the average of tastes. . . . The creators of popular culture are not a sovereign group of "unacknowledged legislators." They work for Hooper ratings to give people what they want. (1957, p. 519)

The Moralizers' Approach to Mass Culture. Broadly speaking, the moralizers do not distinguish between the "social" and the "cultural" issues of a mass society. For them, the problem of maintaining and generating the proper value-commitments is of the same piece as that of maintaining and generating the proper standards of cultural taste. In either case, the problem resides in the assertion of individual responsibility. Unlike the elitists, however, the moralizers do not believe that any special class or group of persons is intrinsically more qualified or has more responsibility than individuals in general. Their analysis is, indeed, more "democratic," but they do not go along with the reformers in believing that the individual is the victim of low-grade supply. Like the elitists, they believe that it is the individual's own fault if he succumbs to it or does not demand better. Again, he gets what he wants and deserves.

The Reformers' Approach to Mass Culture.—Here, of course, the assumptions are reversed. Mass culture is the result of the *loss of consumer sovereignty*: the masses do not get what they want but are "oversold." They are seen as consumers coerced either by the producers of mass culture (variously conceived as the bourgeoisie, Madison Avenue, etc.) or by the very nature of the market itself. (The interesting shift of opprobrium from Wall Street to Madison Avenue will be discussed in Chapter 10.) Their innate capacity to assert the proper standards is taken for granted and is seen as frustrated by the conditions of mass society itself.

The central proposition about the nature of these conditions is what Kornhauser termed the loss of community, or alienation. As Macdonald puts it:

The mass man is a solitary atom, uniform with and undifferentiated from thousands and millions of other atoms who go to make up "the lonely crowd," as David Riesman well calls American society. A folk or a people, however, is a community, i. e., a group of individuals linked to each other by common interests, work, traditions, values, and sentiments; something like a family, each of whose members has a special place and function as an individual while at the same time sharing the group's interests. . . . The scale is small enough so that it "makes a difference" what the individual does, a first condition for human—as against mass—existence. (1957, pp. 69-70)

The argument, already familiar to us, is that the loss of meaningful ties and the sense of purposelessness engendered by alienation incapacitates the individual so that he cannot choose for himself. Mass culture is said to aid and abet this incapacity by presenting him with an homogenized product —easy to understand, escapist in nature, and with the reactions he is supposed to have already built in so that he does not have to think for himself. He is a passive spectator who absorbs mass culture without having to relate to anyone else. Nothing, it seems, atomizes quite so thoroughly as radio and television.

Radio set and telescreen become transformed into a negative family table; the family into a miniature audience. . . . The only thing the members of a family do together—though never as an integrated family group—is to take excursions into a realm of unreality, a world they actually share with no one (for they themselves do not actually share in it). . . . (Anders, 1956, pp. 16-17)

Even when, driven by the lack of meaning in his life, modern man turns to mass culture for distraction, his need is not filled; instead, it is increased. A vicious circle is set in motion.

Far from dispelling unrest, all the (admittedly slim) evidence now on hand suggests that mass culture exacerbates it. Once understood, this fact cuts the ground from under those who justify organized distraction by claiming that it satisfies a fundamental need. Dwight Macdonald comes much closer to the point when he says that it *exploits* that need. (Bernard Rosenberg, 1957, p. 7)

Van den Haag likens mass culture to Freud's notion of dream-work: both produce "substitute gratifications" in order to distract the audience or sleeper (the audience *qua* sleeper?) from reality (1957, pp. 532-33). Habitual recourse to substitute gratifications incapacitates the individual for "real" ones.

Allegedly incapacitated by alienation from making autonomous choice, the masses are "readily available for mobilization," as Kornhauser puts it. They are ready to have standards set for them. The most radical position is along Marxian lines: mass culture is a sop thrown to the masses to lull them into acquiescence, like circuses for the Roman mob. Another interpretation, considerably more popular at present, views the advertising industry—symbolized by "Madison Avenue"—as responsible for setting all the standards. Less concerned with the effect on the public than was an allegedly conspiratorial bourgeoisie and more interested in making profits, the "merchants of discontent," as Packard refers to them, manipulate the public to want things it does not need.

An alternative explanation sees the source of evil as inherent in the nature of the market itself. First, lower quality sells better than higher quality and therefore standards are subverted to the exigencies of the market.

The value of fun is determined by its success on the market, not by anything which could be measured in human terms. (Fromm, 1955b, p. 136)

[Standards are vulgarized by] the effort of a mass medium to hold a mass audience by gauging its appeal to the lowest common denominator of aesthetic receptivity. (Emerson secundus, 1950, p. 138)

Second, an improved technology provides the market with mechanisms that enable it further to maximize the quantity sold at the expense of quality. New technological means of transmitting culture widens the audience; as the audience grows larger, the "common denominator" of demand sinks even lower. In addition, many people who were formerly insulated from mass culture are brought into its sphere of influence—for example, many who rarely read will watch television. Even those who did read are likely to abandon reading, the argument goes, once they can take their pleasure with less effort.

Bernard Rosenberg goes goes so far as to suggest the following:

If one can hazard a single positive formulation (in the form of a hypothesis) it would be that modern technology is the necessary and sufficient cause of mass culture. Neither national character nor the economic arrangement nor the political system has any final bearing on this question. All that really matters is the most recent industrial revolution. (1957, p. 12)

The pseudonymous Emerson secundus does not feel constrained to limit consideration of the technological threat to recent times but draws the line, somewhat ambivalently, at writing itself. Although writing "transmuted barbarism into civilization," he says, "we must now revise our estimates of technological advance in communication; for each new development in the art of communication seems to have broadened the base of culture on the one hand and to have vulgarized the arts on the other" (1950, p. 137).

"Emerson's" comment about the vulgarization of the arts brings us back to the means-ends problem; in this case, technological means, instead of serving cultural ends, become ends in themselves. Preoccupation with technology, as in 3-D, stereo sound, or hi-fi, becomes a substitute for concern over quality of content. Dwight Macdonald suggests that the esthetic virtue of a medium may be related to its technological shortcomings. In a discussion of cinematic art, he approves of Rudolf Arnheim's thesis that "the very properties that make photography and film fall short of perfect reproduction can act as necessary molds of an artistic medium" (1958b). Therefore, although movies may be more entertaining than in the past, they are—since the coming of sound—"no longer an art form."

Although Macdonald is quite clearly talking about esthetic standards in the above instance, most discussions by intellectuals about the "lowering of cultural standards" do not usually distinguish between esthetic and moral standards. Statements about the esthetic quality of high culture and the lack of it in mass culture are intermingled with statements about the moral standards for which the culture serves as a model, with the latter as a direct consequence of the former. However sophisticated the canons of contemporary criticism may be about the analytical independence of these two aspects, the general mass-culture discussion seems to follow a line reminiscent of Ruskin's notion of the moral esthetic. Thus Milton Klonsky writes:

Comic strips, pulp fiction, movies, radio serials, commercial jazz and the rest are a direct result of modern technology and public education [another base-broadening mechanism] . . . they usurp the functions of traditional art in setting the styles, the manners, the images, the standards and goals of life for millions, almost as though they were the organs of an un-official state religion. (1949, p. 349)

The underlying assumption about the consequence of a too open market and a too effective technology is that standards *cannot* be maintained under such conditions. Macdonald has articulated this proposition very clearly by applying Gresham's law—the notion that cheap money drives out good money. Why is it, he asks, that mass culture, while borrowing from and corrupting the contents of both high and folk culture, is able to run off the market those superior forms to which it is indebted?

There seems to be a Gresham's law in cultural as well as monetary circulation: bad stuff drives out the good, since it is more easily understood and enjoyed. It is this facility of access which at once sells *kitsch* [mass culture] on a wide market and also prevents it from achieving quality. (1957, p. 6)

Seen in these terms, the market becomes the "inflationary" one we have described with *both* overspending and overselling and with the value of standards depreciating. Regardless of whether low quality of demand *or* low quality of supply and lack of consumer sovereignty started the downward spiral, once it is set in motion, one side stimulates the other. Standards drop, if they do not disappear altogether. Macdonald summarizes this position:

I see mass culture as a reciprocating engine, and who is to say, once it has been set in motion, whether the stroke or the counterstroke is "responsible" for its continued action. (1957, pp. 71-2)

Starting out on the structure-oriented side of the analysis, Arthur Schlesinger, Jr. fears the same conclusion and predicts as a possibility the state of affairs that Ortega assumed from the beginning:

By concentrating on the lowest common denominator, they [mass communications] may in time create the very uniform unleavened mass which is already the postulate of their activiites. (1953, p. 164)

An Alternative View

6

Social Change and the Problems of Choice

I am indebted to Dwight Macdonald for suggesting that a Gresham's law—"the cheap drives out the good"—is operating in mass culture. If what he and others have been telling us about American society is correct, then Gresham's law is a vivid metaphorical formulation of what is happening. In describing a situation where standards are unstable, it joins the issue—not only between the intellectuals' point of view and mine but between the two wings of intellectual ideology as well.

The moralizers attribute the instability of standards to a decline of values that has come about because members of the society have failed to live up to them. It views the maintenance of values as depending primarily on individual affirmation of them. Loss of values is due to loss of individualism. And loss of individualism equals an increase in conformity. This approach seems to be saying that the individual's posture toward society (which is understood as the social pressures of other people) can be either individualistic or conforming, or a mixture of both. But this approach also implies that the *more* the individual gives in to social pressures by conforming, the *less* "individualistic" he is. The logic of this formulation is often called a zero-sum concept: there is a fixed quantity of choices available so that what one side gains the other inevitably loses.

To pursue Macdonald's metaphor further, one might say

that there are two kinds of standards, or "currencies," "equal in debt-paying power but unequal in intrinsic value"—as *Webster's Collegiate Dictionary* puts it in defining Gresham's law—individualism and conformity. Instead of risking the former and more valuable, it is hoarded; the "market," then, is flooded with the latter and becomes unstable.

Instability of standards, from this point of view, is graphically illustrated in Riesman's account of the other-directed peer-group, where standards of behavior are in such a constant state of flux that the other-directed person is hard-pressed to keep up with what he is supposed to conform to. In the face of rapidly fluctuating tastes and styles, conformity and the social approval it elicits are the only standard. Such a "currency" is indeed subject to rapid devaluation when individualism fails to stabilize its value.

Along the same lines, the elitist interpretation of mass culture attributes the instability of standards to a loss of guidance from the elite. Their standards represent the more valuable "currency," but it has been driven off the market by the lower standards, or cheaper currency, of the tastes of the masses.

The reformers locate standards in the organic community, where the individual can know them at first hand in meaningful relations. But alienation arising from the division of labor has destroyed that basis of evaluation, producing alienation, or estrangement from self. As alienated man becomes a commodity on the labor market, his alienated personality also becomes a commodity on the social market. As in the case of conformity, the standards that govern the selling of commodities are a considerable comedown from those that prevailed before. In mass culture, too, loss of community has meant loss of folk culture. Folk standards, stable in each community, diversified from one another, have given way to the uniform yet unstable mass standards.

But instability of standards, according to the intellectuals, does not pervade the entire range of human activities. In certain areas, particularly those in which the "human" quality is regarded as highly questionable, standards are all too unequivocal. Standards of efficiency in economic production and in bureaucratic organization are firmly entrenched. Scientific and technological criteria have priority, no matter what ends they may be serving. In terms, again, of a zero-sum concept, the ascendancy and increased stability of these standards necessitates decline and instability for others. At the cultural level, the alleged priority given to the empirical-rational aspects of meaning detracts from the emphasis on evaluative aspects (the more science, the less humanities) and on artistic aspects (the more technology, the less art). At the level of society, the alleged priority given to productivity and organization detracts from the emphasis on human needs; the "system" ("everything is just too big these days") is running along—if not running away—on its own standards at the expense of individual decision (the more "system," the less individual autonomy).

On the basis of these arguments, the intellectuals conclude that the past has failed to deliver what should have been the future; we are stuck—at least for the present if not for all time—with a society that is not even as good as it *could* have been (not to mention how good it *ought* to be). The paramount issue, it seems to me, in these arguments is the nature of the changes that have been going on in the society. Have these changes in fact brought about the consequences attributed to them?

Whether explicit or not, the intellectuals' "theory" of social change seems to be based on the two assumptions of Gresham's law and a zero-sum concept. That is to say, when two standards of choice are available, the "cheaper," or less desirable, drives out the "better," or more desirable. And what the "cheaper" standard gains, the "better" standard inevitably loses. Although this kind of change may indeed occur in a society, it by no means exhausts all of the possibilities for social change. Another theory of social change is necessary in order to account for the phenomena that are clearly observable in American society.

Change as Structural Differentiation

The most appropriate model, in my opinion, for analyzing the kind of change that we are concerned with here is that of *evolution*: differentiation of structure and specialization of function and the complementary processes of reintegration. In *The Division of Labor in Society*, Durkheim used this model as the foundation for his theory of social change. In doing so, he sharply criticized Spencer's utilitarian notion that society was somehow built up from an aggregate of individuals with "given" wants or needs—a point of view that has many conceptual similarities with the moralizers' approach. He also presented the argument that increases in social organization (through the division of labor) result in positive increases for individual opportunity. He challenged the notion that this process inevitably leads to an insect-type society for human beings—a notion that the reformers tend to embrace.

According to Durkheim, a society is conceived of as a system, which—by definition—is made up of component parts, or structures, that are related to one another with some degree of determinacy, or order. The degree of order that actually exists is always open to question and cannot be taken for granted by assuming, as one branch of utilitarian thought did, that order is supplied "automatically" by a natural identity of interests. But if an actual society does in fact exist over a period of time, it is managing somehow to feed and govern its people, to prevent them from killing each other off, to bring up its young—in short, to maintain some degree of order. When confronted with the evidence that such a society has over time maintained its identity as a system, the analyst must explain why it has not fallen apart; he must account for whatever order is actually present. This is another way of saying that determinate relationships do in fact exist and that whatever happens among the component

parts cannot be random. Such determinacy is not an "all-
or-none" principle; although one cannot predict with certainty what will happen to the society, neither can one
say—in the face of a particular pattern of relationships—that
it can go in any direction whatsoever.

All societies, no matter how simple or complex, must fulfill certain basic requirements—producing and allocating resources (at the minimum, food and shelter), ensuring some
degree of conformity from its members, controlling deviance,
and the like. In this connection, Durkheim used the term
"function." Function does not mean just any process (the
action that takes place among the different parts) going on
in the society, it means process in terms of its relation to
meeting the requirements of the system (Durkheim, 1949,
p. 49)—e.g., industrial production is a process that fills an
economic function.

Thus all societies must fulfill a set of basic functions—
however frugally or prodigally the needs are met. The central
problem of analysis is to work out the relationship between
structures (the component parts of the society) and functions. Are all functions being performed by one structure?
Or is the system so highly differentiated that each of many
structures, instead of having to perform several functions
at once, can specialize in performing one only? These two
alternatives pose limiting cases, each extreme being actually
highly unlikely. In analyzing a particular case, the problem
is to discover what its degree of structural differentiation is.

In a relatively simple society, several different functions
are performed by single structures. A kinship clan, for example, will perform political, economic, religious, and familial
functions. In such a case, no one function can be carried
out independently of all the others. The relationships that
exist among the members of the clan permeate the performance of all functions. A's economic relation to B is at
the same time political, religious, and so on. Since kinship
is the basis of such a system, the flexibility of the structure
is even further limited by the fact of biological relatedness;

age, sex, and birth order determine who fills A's role—he is, for example, mother's brother, or eldest son.

When two or more functions are performed by the same structure, they are *ascribed* to each other, that is, the performance of one is "tied to," or dependent on, the performance of the others; the conditions and limitations of one are the conditions and limitations of all.

In addition, the performance of each function requires its own type of resources: e.g., economic functions require capital and labor; political functions must recruit loyalty and support. In a society with a high degree of ascription (which is another way of saying a low degree of structural differentiation), the resources required for different functions cannot be generated independently of one another. Thus, in the classical peasant society, the labor force available to work the fields depends largely on the number of children born and reared in the family.

As structural differentiation occurs within a society, functional specialization also occurs. When two functions, previously performed by the same structure, are subsequently performed by two newly differentiated structures, each function, under favorable conditions, can be fulfilled more effectively than before. The decisions made in carrying out one function and the recruitment of the necessary resources for it can be effected independently of the other. The biological analogy, on which Durkheim (1949) drew, is obvious. In an amoeba, one cell does everything; in a human being, the biological division of labor is exceedingly complex: the increase in total functional capacity is considerable.

A pertinent illustration from American society is that of the structural differentiation between firm and family. The following discussion contrasts the farm—where family and firm are "fused" in the same structure—with the case where the head of the household is *employed* outside the home. (The family-firm, where it is operated as a business outside the home, represents an intermediate stage of differentiation.) Before these two structures were differentiated, as in the case of the family farm (a century ago well over half the American population lived and worked on farms), both economic and familial functions were carried out by the same structure. When firm was differentiated from family: 1) the segregation of place of residence from that of work meant that the managerial control of each became independent from that of the other. The family no longer had to be run like a business; the business no longer had to concern itself with family problems. 2) The financing of the firm became independent of the financing of the household. Decisions about spending money on plant or equipment no longer had to be weighed against decisions about spending money on food, clothing, and education. 3) The recruitment of the labor force for the firm was no longer ascribed to family membership. The firm could recruit the services of those who might be better qualified than family members for its operations, and the sons of the family were no longer obliged to follow their father's occupational role.

C. Wright Mills, speaking nostalgically of an agrarian past, quotes R. H. Tawney to the effect that "it is a quietness to a man's mind to live upon his own [farm] and to know his heir certain" (1951, p. 1). That may be fine for dad, but, we are at least entitled to ask, what about the son?

By means of such differentiation, resources become more mobile. There are many other examples. The differentiation of the corporation from the family-firm has meant that the resource of capital—now largely generated by "plowing back" earnings—could be emancipated from the necessity of individual family savings. The emergence of labor unions has helped to bring about the emancipation of the interests of labor from ascription to a particular firm. The rise of public education has meant that the training of children can be carried on independently of the resources—both financial and cultural—of the family. The differentiation of "pure" research from applied research has meant that advances in knowledge can be emancipated from ascription to particular practical problems.

   As these resources become more mobile, they can be combined together in a greater variety of ways. Their recruitment
and utilization is less tied to other considerations. With
specialization, the performance of a particular function can
be carried out more intensely than where several functions
must be considered. The dentist, for example, can spend
more time improving his knowledge and skill if he does not
have to raise his own food and tan his own leather. In addition, the range of human choice is greatly increased, as we
shall see. This is what is meant by increases in functional
capacity.
   A graphic example from economic production—where these
principles are more easily illustrated—will indicate what is
involved in the combination of resources. From 1929 to
1957, the Office of Business Economics tells us:

. . . the physical amount of capital applied in manufacturing production virtually doubled, whereas the number of man-hours worked
increased by two-fifths. In other words, over this period the amount
of capital per man-hour increased more than one-third. This increased application of capital of improved efficiency has been a big
factor in the growth of manufacturing production, which in 1957
had risen to 2½ times its 1929 volume. The fact that the expansion
of output in manufacturing significantly outstripped that in either
labor or capital underscores the importance of the other factors
noted above. . . . (1958, p. 3)

   The factors noted were technological and managerial progress, a high-rate of capital formation, advances in education
and skills of the working population, the shifting of the
working force into activities where production is relatively
high, and the economies of large-scale production and the
increased division of labor—in short, the generation of resources that could be mobilized and fluidly combined through
organization.
   To summarize Durkheim's analysis of social change, the
central proposition is that *structural differentiation emancipates resources from ascriptive ties and increases functional
capacity.* It is a way of explaining changes that may or may
not occur. It does not claim that such a process of develop-

ment is in any way inevitable; the loosening of ascriptive ties, for example, requires a definite departure from established traditions—one aspect of such a departure is what Weber called "rationalization." We have already touched on this topic but we can now define it further by saying that rationalization consists in breaking down the ascription of means to ends. The pursuit of given ends becomes emancipated from ascription to fixed, traditional means. Newer means of attaining ends, if more effective, may replace existing means; the principle of change in this respect becomes legitimated.

Moreover, this departure from a traditional, ascriptive base can occur only in the presence of certain necessary conditions. Perhaps the most familiar of these is the requisite technology; indeed, this condition is so conspicuous that many interpreters believe it to be the *only* causal factor (just as Bernard Rosenberg, referred to a few pages ago, believes that technology is "the necessary and sufficient cause of mass culture"). Max Weber's work, however, pointed out that other conditions besides technology are also necessary. He emphasized the importance of certain types of values—especially the commitments of individuals to those values—as necessary to give impetus to change. His example was the role of the Protestant Ethic, as a type of necessary value-commitment, in the development of Western capitalism. Similarly, McClelland and his collaborators (1953) have emphasized another type of condition necessary for a break with traditional ways of doing things in what they call the need-for-achievement as part of the personality make-up.

This theoretical model of change does not claim that structural differentiation occurs in the same way in every case. It may be "introduced," so to speak, at widely varying points in the social structure. The contrast between the American and Soviet Union cases is a dramatic example. Nor are all industrialized societies necessarily equally differentiated. Although the Soviet Union bears important resemblances to American society in its industrial organization, it is a serious (and common) mistake to regard the two societies as essentially similar just because they are both industrialized; for in the Soviet Union, the economic, legal, and educational structures are not differentiated from the political structure to anywhere near the extent that they are in American society.

We will be particularly concerned with two consequences that structural differentiation may have for a society: *extensity* and *upgrading*.

Although differentiation may proceed to rather high levels of complexity, it by no means necessarily takes place throughout the entire society; some sectors may become highly differentiated while others remain considerably less so, at the same time. The structure of American business firms is a case in point, having large corporate structures (where ownership, fiduciary control, managerial control, and labor are all differentiated from one another) and small family firms (where family members run the business with no paid employees) side by side. *Extensity* in other words, *refers to the degree to which differentiation permeates all structures of the same class.*

The increase in functional capacity that comes about through differentiation places greater demands for performance on the society as a whole as well as on its individual members. Compare, for example, what must be learned by members of a subsistence society with that necessary in a highly industrialized one. *Upgrading* refers to this *increase in demands for performance.* The impact of upgrading on different parts of the structure, however, is not evenly distributed; greater demands may be made on some parts and less on others.

The changes that structural differentiation brings about in a society usually cause serious disturbances, or what we have called *strains*, along the way—but again, unevenly in location and intensity. When differentiation occurs, the problem of integrating the relations between the differentiated parts must be worked out. Resources (including human resources) that were formerly pre-empted by one structural unit must now be allocated among two or more; hence, new standards of allocation have to be formulated. The relationship of the newly differentiated structures to the rest of the society must be reorganized. Above all, the expectations of the members of society involved must be restructured to fit the newly emerging social patterns. They have to make distinctions that previously were unnecessary. Until such reorganization with its new standards and expectations is attained, some degree of uncertainty is bound to prevail, often resulting in human suffering. Whether or not the "growing pains" are worth it is an evaluative question of costs, but it is a matter of historical record that the development of societies from a non-literate base cannot take place without them.

In the first chapter we considered ideology to be one type of reaction to strain. We will proceed, then, to analyze the current strain as a consequence of the structural differentiation that American society is undergoing and to analyze ideology as an attempt to understand those changes in its own terms. The present ideological issue centers on the relation of the individual to society. The society, it is alleged, exerts undue pressures on the individual; or, conversely, the individual surrenders to them. Furthermore, the intellectuals conceive of society in this instance as primarily "other people" with whom the individual interacts in various groups. We will be concerned with the roles that the individual plays in these groups. Since the main ideological preoccupation is with social pressures and conformity, we will be concerned with the impact of these various roles in groups on the individual. (We shall turn later to the related problem of mass culture.)

A Few Facts

With the rapid structural differentiation that American society has undergone even within the last few decades, Americans have become increasingly involved in taking on a number of differentiated roles—particularly those that have taken them out of the home, that have become emancipated from ascriptive ties. The following data illustrate some of the lines of development, particularly the growth in extensity as differentiation spreads to include increasing proportions of the population.

The predominant impact of these changes on individuals is in their occupational roles. Today, a larger proportion of persons of working-force age have occupational roles differentiated from any connection with the household. The rise has been due mainly to the decline in agriculture (from over one out of four in the labor force in 1920 to less than one out of eleven in 1959) and the increase in the number of women in the labor force (from slightly more than one out of five in 1920 to over one out of three in 1958). In addition, a considerable proportion of workers is employed by large-scale organization (which in the nature of the case is highly differentiated). Of all those in 1956 working for *private* non-farm firms excluding professional services, three out of eight worked for firms that employed a thousand persons or more. In addition, the proportion working for government (all levels), another large-scale employer, has increased from one out of fourteen members of the labor force in 1930 to almost one out of six in 1958. (All data are from *Statistical Abstract of the United States 1959* unless otherwise noted.) The proliferation of governmental regulatory agencies, particularly since the days of the New Deal, is in itself a sensitive index of the increasing complexity of the society.

Beyond the occupational aspects of the society, sheer increase in numbers—as the intellectuals rightly point out (the population has increased from 123 million in 1930 to about 180 million in 1960)—has intensified the necessity of "coping with" other people and consequently has increased their interdependence on one another. In the one decade from 1940 to 1950, the numbers living in what the Census people call Standard Metropolitan Areas (a county or group of contiguous counties having at least one city of 50,000 persons or more) increased over 22 per cent. In 1950, one out of every four Americans lived in twelve urbanized areas of a million inhabitants or more (Hatt and Riess, 1951, p. 62).

The increase in suburban residence—from sixteen million in 1930 to over thirty million in 1953 (Editors of Fortune, 1955, p. 270)—has necessitated the rapid social organization of new swelling communities, particularly for providing educational facilities for the "war babies." Although I cannot cite the figures, I believe there is little doubt that there has been a considerable increase in community participation addressed to solving these problems—more differentiated roles for members of the society to assume. Indeed, if we can believe what Whyte (1956) and others tell us about suburban living, the suburbanites are virtually run ragged keeping up with these obligations.

Other non-occupational roles have increased. Trade union membership has grown from one out of five persons in non-agricultural employment in 1939 to one out of three in 1953. Church membership (gentile only) rose from 49 per cent in 1940 to 61 per cent in 1957. There is a wide participation in voluntary associations—clubs, societies, lodges, fraternities. Bell (1956, p. 80) says that in 1956 there were at least two hundred thousand of them with a membership of close to eighty million men and women. A significant rise in the proportion of persons who are married (significant in the sense that being married entails taking on new roles—that of spouse and usually of parent) has occurred: from 1940 to 1954 the proportion of males fourteen years and over who were single (and had always been single) dropped from 35 to 23 per cent; for females, from 28 to 18 per cent (Glick, 1957, p. 104).

Even among the young, differentiation has been going on as agencies outside the home play an increasingly important part in their lives. From 1950 to 1958, the proportion of five-year-olds going to kindergarten rose from 31 to 49 per cent (Bureau of the Census, 1959b). From 1940 to 1958 the number of Boy Scouts more than tripled and that of Girl

Scouts quintupled (while the population in the five-to-nine-teen-year-old group increased by less than half). In addition, young people have taken on occupational roles (predominantly part-time jobs) while in school. In 1940, only four per cent of high-school age children were labor force members (unemployment, however, was high in that year). But from 1947 to 1956 (years in which unemployment was at about the same level), the proportion of students aged fourteen to seventeen who were in the labor force rose from 17 to 23 per cent (Bureau of the Census, 1957).

Differentiation has produced an upgrading of the demands made on individuals in roles—that is to say, of the levels of performance required of them. Since upgrading is more easily demonstrated in the case of occupational roles than it is for other roles, let us look at the record in that respect. Kaplan and Casey (1958) show that at the higher levels, the proportion of persons in professional and technical occupations has increased from 1930 to 1959 from 6.8 to 11.8 per cent; it has almost doubled. In managerial, official, and entrepreneurial occupations the proportion increased from 7.4 to 11.6 per cent. The percentage of persons working as craftsmen, foremen, and the like, has remained relatively stable at about 12.5 per cent.

At the lower levels, the proportion working as "operatives" (generally considered semi-skilled labor) has increased slightly from 1930 to 1959—from 15.8 to 17.7 per cent (due to more extensive industrialization), but during the shorter more recent period an upward trend for this class of occupation has been reversed—presumably as a result of greater applications of technology. Thus, the percentage of persons working as operatives reached a high of 21 per cent in 1948 and has steadily decreased since that time. But on the lowest end of the scale, there has been a sharp reduction of non-farm laborers doing unskilled work. From 1930 to 1959, the proportion dropped from 11 to 4.6 per cent.

The proportion of clerical and sales workers here has increased from 15.2 (1930) to 22.1 (1959) per cent. It is difficult to appraise this type of work in terms of the level of performance required because it is a catch-all for a wide range of jobs—some of them demanding high levels of performance, others relatively routine. One can, however, make a qualitative distinction about the kinds of demands made on persons holding these jobs: their work entails, above all, dealing with other people rather than things. It is characterized by social interdependence and a complexity of role-relationships. Thus, the increase in this sector at least represents an extension of social differentiation, however problematical the upgrading may be.

Beyond the record of the past few decades, there is almost universal consensus that this process of upgrading will be continued—even at an accelerated rate—and that practically all jobs will require higher levels of educational preparation. Particularly salient is the rapidly expanding demand for scientists, engineers, and technicians in industry (not to mention the concomitant demand for persons trained to educate them) as advances in electronics, atomic energy, and automation are increasingly applied. In 1957, one out of every thirty-two persons in the labor force already fell in this category; whereas in 1940 only one out of a hundred did. In 1957, for the first time in history, there were more mathematicians in industry than there were in colleges and universities; they had doubled since 1954, just three years before (Bureau of Labor Statistics, 1959).

The increasing need for highly specialized personnel, not only in scientific areas but others as well, means that decisions can no longer be reached by one man alone. No matter how rugged an individualist the boss may be, he must depend on others for information and for judgment on matters about which he himself cannot, in the nature of the case, know very much. The old-style straight-line authority can no longer prevail. Moreover, the way in which each specialist presents his information and the kinds of questions he must answer depend on his fitting the information in with that of other specialists. Individual contributions cannot be measured ahead of time and tossed in independently of each other, like baking a cake. Thus, interdependence and working in groups is increasingly necessary, at some level of decision.

Problems in Interpreting Structural Differentiation

With this core of facts before us, let us turn to the problem of understanding what this process of differentiation has meant for the individual. As the figures readily reveal, the changes have involved him in increasingly complex relations with other people. We will now examine the ideological interpretations of these changes—in particular the many questions ideologists have raised about "freedom versus authority," "independence versus dependence," and "wholeness versus alienation." In doing so, we will use Durkheim's theory of social change as the framework for an alternative interpretation. The conceptual difficulties involved in interpreting social change are formidable enough by themselves, but they are made even more so in view of the specific strains and urgent problems that lead to its investigation.

The Problem of Choice.—A human action can be looked at as a choice among perceived alternatives. Choice necessarily implies a standard of selection: why choose x when the choice of x requires the rejection of y and z?

Unless one wants to adopt the utilitarian position of assuming that such choices are made on the basis of individual criteria alone, a major source of criteria lies in the normative order of society, the shared expectations of what is considered desirable. (Parsons and White, 1961)

Order, then, may be said to exist when standards are not applied randomly by individuals (or other acting units) but are shared so that A's choice can be made in expectation of B's, and vice versa.

No real system, obviously, is completely ordered. Situations are constantly arising where standards applicable to them have not yet been established (particularly in complex societies; less so in traditional ones). In such cases, they may be said to be dealt with on an *ad hoc* basis. If situations of a similar nature arise frequently enough and with sufficient intensity, the *ad hoc* solutions tend to become established as generalized procedures. What previously had to be solved afresh at each recurrence comes to be dealt with automatically in terms of newly established standards. In this way, the level of normative order is raised. We speak of the building up of such order in society as *institutionalization*.

The predominant means of building up order in modern society and reducing recurring *ad hoc* solutions is through the legal system—by legislating new standards as required (e.g., establishing arbitration procedures), or—as in common law—by referring to and developing from precedent. Indeed, citing precedent may be thought of as generalizing the *ad hoc* solution of a particular situation to others of its kind. The existence of order means that action is predictable in general terms. This does not mean that one can predict how any particular action is going to come out, but that he knows how to go about making choices in terms of what others will do—he knows what the procedures are. Uncertainty exists in situations where such order has not yet been established; people are faced with choices for which they have inadequate guidance and must pursue a course of action without knowing what to expect. Durkheim called this lack of adequate guidance, of normative definition, *anomie*.

Because order is characterized by the fact that standards of choice are *shared* with others, in the nature of the case, choice is restricted to some extent in any society. A cannot make *any* choice he wants because he must consider B's choices as well. In view of this restriction, the building up of order in a complex society is frequently interpreted as a narrowing of the range of choices. It is stated that the more one must consider an increasing number of other persons, the less freedom he has to act on his own. It is this interpretation that is at the very center of the ideological aversion to social interaction in a complex society; those who plead for "individualism" say the restriction is not necessary, and those who talk about "alienation" say it is forcibly imposed on man. Since the latter interpretation is somewhat more sophisticated about social structure than the former (although not, in my opinion, about its implications for choice), the following comments will be addressed primarily to the problems that the reformers have concentrated on, although other issues will be raised along the way.

We are already familiar with the reformers' strictures about the restriction of choice. The alienated laborer cannot decide what products to make, what tasks to perform, at what pace he wants to work, and so on. Similar restrictions pervade the entire society as dependence on others mounts. There are four traps in this line of reasoning. The first pair is characterized by the fallacy of the zero-sum concept and the second pair by confusion about the level of generality.

The first fallacy is that of *fixed quantity of choices:* the notion that in any society the number of choices decreases as the division of labor rises. Specialization, it is claimed, means not only doing one thing instead of many but the necessity of having to do that one thing in accordance with what others do. With sufficient complexity, or "social dependence," all freedom of choice practically vanishes so that *no* one has it— hence, anonymous authority. This fallacy overlooks the fact that more choices are made available as differentiation progresses; there is an increase in the functional capacity of the system. It is not a closed system and the quantity of choices is not fixed.

The second fallacy is that of *limitation of choice through competition:* the notion that differentiated structural units or even differentiated functions are in conflict with each other because they compete for the same resources. With alienation, we are told, laborers increasingly compete with each other for jobs; what one gains the other loses.

This fallacy ignores Durkheim's observation that specialization reduces competition. In terms of the labor market, the more specialized jobs there are, the less competition; dentists do not compete for jobs with carpenters. No one would claim that competition does not exist, but this is true of even the simplest society. In a completely agricultural society, there is intense competition for the most desirable plots of ground. When we speak of a modern society as being more "competitive" than a simpler one, we are talking about a considerably higher level of expectations and rewards.

This line of reasoning, however, has more far-reaching implications in less obvious contexts with regard to differentiated structures or functions of a dissimilar nature. Thus, in maintaining the balance between work and recreation, the moralizers aver that increased hedonism necessarily results in the decline of the Protestant Ethic; there seems to be a fixed quantity of action so that if one plays more he must be working less. This may be true in terms of hours spent, but time spent is not by itself an adequate measure of the amount of work or play engaged in, for it fails to take account of the intensity of the activity.

As previously noted, it is in the nature of differentiation that functions can be carried out more fully when they become structurally separated. There may be more "hedonism" in the suburban home—more enjoyment of children, more "goods" consumed—than was the case on the old family farm, but this fact does not necessarily detract from work done in structurally differentiated contexts. Indeed, differentiation makes the distinction between the two sharper.

The present argument is also relevant to the reformers' assumption about conflict between standards; namely, that as standards of efficiency and productivity become more dominant, standards pertaining to human values decline— again, an either-or choice. This assumption is based not only on a zero-sum fallacy (the more of one, the less of the other) but is also linked to "Gresham's law." The implicit line of reasoning is that, assuming a Gresham's law operates, we can state *which* standard of choice, resource, or whatever, will *gain* and which one will *lose*. With such an assumption, the obvious conclusion is that the standard of less intrinsic value will gain and the more valuable will decline ("gain" or "decline" in terms of use, not in terms of value—"the cheap drives out the good"). By this line of reasoning, the intellectuals often seem to analyze social change purely in terms of zero-sum processes and Gresham's law (see page 72).

This conclusion overlooks the fact that by means of structural differentiation standards are sorted out from one another and applied in different fields of social interaction. Since the standard that predominates in one field does not directly "compete" with that in another field, the application of a Gresham's law is not justified in this case. The two "currencies" are not circulating in the same "market." That standards have become more clearly differentiated is a more correct statement; economic, political, and religious procedures of action are more clearly differentiated than they were—to take an extreme illustration—in the ritual gift-exchange in non-literate societies. However, they have become so only as the fields of social interaction to which they apply have been differentiated as well. Such differentiation demands, of course, increased sophistication of members of the society (if not of social critics) to discriminate among situations in choosing appropriate standards. And this demand on individuals is one of the important sources of strain.

To return to the intellectuals' contention that as the (less desirable) standards of productivity and efficiency gain ground, other (more desirable) standards decline, the family is again a case in point. Where the family structure is differentiated from economic activities and does not have to manage a farm or firm, it is not governed by standards of efficiency. It is quite justifiable to question, as Galbraith has done, the allocation of certain resources to the production of consumers' goods. But the question of whether the standard of productivity itself is receiving too much emphasis requires a careful definition of the meaning of "productivity" and of the implications of the standard for the rest of the society. A high level of *economic* productivity cannot simply be interpreted without qualification as forcing similar standards on all other types of social interaction. It does not follow that an increased emphasis in this direction means that the individual must be more economically productive and efficient at home with the family. Indeed, since high productivity often shortens working hours, he may have greater freedom to apply other standards off the job.

Further, the term productivity itself tends to be slippery. In the broadest sense, not all productivity is purely economic nor concerned with generating consumers' goods. If productivity is intended to make possible the building up of non-economic as well as economic resources, then the statement that there is an emphasis on productivity in American society is quite correct. But this does not mean that *economic* standards have been extrapolated to all the rest of society. Since, historically, the focus of attention has been on developing economic resources, there is a tendency to assume that the production of *all* resources is an extension of the same processes and an application of the same standards.

One may suggest that the intellectuals are speaking metaphorically, but when metaphor becomes the basis for an entire argument instead of an illustration, accurate analysis is not possible. Thus Fromm says, "The mechanism through which the anonymous authority [of peer-groups] operates is conformity" (1955b, p. 153). If by "anonymous authority" he simply means "institutionalized expectations," it isn't news; if, however, he means "authority" to be a precise term, conceptually distinct from normative relationships in general, then he is saying that peer-groups operate like political power-structures in view of the individual's increasing powerlessness (1955b, p. 99). Seeking the fulfillment of personal needs in a peer-group—what Fromm pejoratively refers to as "the need to adjust and be approved of"—even if done in the most slavishly conformist manner, is not carried out in a political context if the term political is to have any meaning at all. Again, we have an extrapolation of standards from one sector of the society to the entire society.

The peer-group, from Fromm's point of view, operates according to standards of power and nothing else.

The third and fourth fallacies arise from *confusion about the level of generality;* that is, from making statements at higher levels of generality while actually referring to lower levels. A ludicrously extreme example will serve based on the observation that men no longer wear detached collars: American values have changed (higher-level statement) because men have changed their evaluation of collar styles (lower-level reference).

The third fallacy results from such a confusion in historical comparison: referring to a more differentiated structure (or function) in the present in terms of a less differentiated one in the past when both have the same name. It is the fallacy of *ignoring the restriction of meaning.* However, semantically pardonable, it is theoretically confusing. Thus, to talk about today's family in terms of the nineteenth-century family is like comparing the right ventricle with the one-chamber heart. Today's "family" is not the same structure as yesterday's "family"; it is more highly specialized and performs fewer functions. It has, of course, "lost functions" (and therefore makes choices in fewer areas of activity), but the lost functions are being fulfilled in other parts of the society. Because of this change, the members of the more specialized family play more specialized roles. The father who goes off to business is not comparable with the father who was both head of family *and* of firm at the same time within the same structural context.

Norman Podhoretz has sensitively described this change in father's role from inferences he made while watching family dramas on television. He says, "the father guides and administers his household; he does not rule it . . . he is a constitutional leader rather than an absolute monarch" (1953, p. 536). This formulation bears a remarkable resemblance to Parsons' statement that the father is more of a "chairman of the board" than a manager, a role now assumed by the mother.

In this connection, it is a popular lament today that men

are losing their masculinity and women, their femininity. These qualities, I suspect, are usually defined in terms of what we thought characterized our grandparents, reinforced by nostalgic memories of cuspidors and lavender sachet. Our grandparents, however, played fewer roles in less differentiated structures; they had fewer opportunities to express themselves in a variety of ways, to fill different needs in differentiated social contexts. The man whose role as head of the family combined both being a father and running a family business or farm could not engage in the domestic activities the modern father does without their seeming inappropriate to his responsibility for managing the business. As manager of the business, he was also manager of the home and the woman's role was subordinated to his; "a man was master in his own home." With the range of activities (of choices, if you will) structurally restricted for each sex, the appropriate behavior for each was more highly ascribed to sex. Attribution of masculinity and femininity covered a wider range of behavior.

To define behavior in such terms today would considerably limit the range of what can be considered appropriate; it would be saying that sexual ascription should determine *all* roles—a woman's place is in the home, as the saying goes. With the sharp increase in the proportion of women in the labor force that our data show, it is a common allegation that holding down a job threatens a woman's feminine qualities; she must compete with men, etc. It can also be said, however, that she has new opportunities to behave differently *in differentiated* social contexts that were denied her grandmother. As Margaret Mead, whose interest in this area is well known, once said (on television, I confess), "Today's woman may be less feminine than her grandmother, but she has more opportunities to be a human being" (paraphrased).

Parenthetically, it should be noted that masculinity and femininity are often defined in terms of style of behavior. To some extent, sexually appropriate style is independent of the types of change I have been discussing; thus, in America before the First World War it was considered "effeminate" for men to smoke cigarettes, and "masculine" (if not demimondaine or Bohemian) for women to smoke at all.

The fourth fallacy is that of *ignoring higher levels of choice*: the notion that restriction of choice at a specific level implies the restriction of choice in general. The "alienated" employee of a firm may well have relinquished the choice available to the "unalienated" man (although the range of choice open to the latter bears looking into) of what products he would like to make or services to perform, of what hours he would like to work and with whom. But this is not to say that he does not have more general choices in picking his line of work and in deciding for whom to work.

If the individual is to express his unique personality by developing his own particular productive capacities, as Fromm puts it, he has greater freedom to do so if he is not confronted with problems for which he has little talent and less interest. If individuality is what we want and if we can assume that differences in genetic inheritance, "temperament," and life experience equip individuals with different talents and interests, then specialization, or "alienation," is the best social arrangement to provide opportunities for their expression. The university scholar does not have to face the financial problems of fund raising and investment; the tool-maker does not face the problem of building a plant.

In recommending that workers participate in management and that all men work with both their heads and their hands, some ideologists seem either to assume that everyone *wants* to pursue this range of activities or else that everyone *ought* to. (One wonders just how much variability of choice is available in Fromm's communitarian socialism —cf. *Sane Society*—where "togetherness" is carried out with a vengeance.) It has been the policy of the American labor movement that the rights of labor to some degree of autonomy in work processes (as well as adequate wages and benefits) were best attained by eschewing participation in overall managerial responsibility. This policy is an implicit recognition of functional specialization; it seeks its ends without having to consider problems extraneous to them.

The arguments I have briefly reviewed here are time-worn, but the issues raised by the reformers indicate that the horse we are beating has not yet been pronounced dead. One further point, however, is in order. More often than not, ideological discussions about the alienated laborer take the assembly-line worker as their example: they apotheosize Charlie Chaplin's hero as the martyr of Modern Times. However dreary and inhumane such work may be, it is not the archetypal occupational role in American society. Our data on upgrading demonstrate that the proportion of persons in lower-level jobs is a shrinking minority; with the increased application of cybernetic-type automation, it is practically certain that even greater reductions in routine, mechanical work lie ahead. The technological liberation of human effort from routine drudgery includes clerical work as well and has been going on apace with the increasing use of punch-card systems, automatic filing devices, microfilming techniques, and other business machinery.

There are, in addition, two other areas in which the range of choice is widened by differentiation. Upgrading, particularly at the level of professional and technical specialties, frees the "worker" from submitting to complete authority. Where the old-style straight-line authority can no longer prevail (see page 84), the nature of his individual contribution is not totally subject to hierarchical authority but is made in accordance with the standards and available knowledge of his specialty. Although specialists do compete in securing jobs, they also co-operate in solving technical problems. In view of the indispensability of the specialist to the firm and the nature of the challenge he faces, it cannot simply be said of him that "he cannot realize himself in his work" (Mills, 1951, p. 14); and his numbers are rapidly growing.

Second, whatever restriction of choice the "anonymous authority" of bureaucratic organization may impose on the individual while he is working, it is specifically limited to his occupational role. Office is separated from person, as Weber expressed it. Any statement about the range of choices while working must also be balanced against those available while not working. Unquestionably, the division of labor has overwhelmingly multiplied the latter. The wage-earner (about whom the ideologists are most concerned) works fewer hours (from sixty a week in 1900 to forty a week currently—and thirty-five for most office workers). Income per person (for the entire population), *after* taxes, in *constant* dollars (taking account of inflation) has doubled since 1920 (*Fortune*, 1955, p. 261). Inequality of income continues to be reduced (though gradually): the change that occurred between 1940 and 1950 yielded the greatest relative gains for the lowest-paid occupations and the smallest for the highest-paid (Miller, 1955, p. 5); the distribution of family incomes was less skewed in the direction of the lower incomes in 1957 than it was only ten years previously (Office of Business Economics, 1958, p. 45). The percentage of families living in homes they themselves owned has increased from 43 per cent in 1940 to 60 per cent in 1956 (Bureau of the Census, 1959a).

These data are not intended as a part of the "American celebration" or as a defense of the status quo. They are presented merely to indicate that the alienated worker's "loss of freedom" while at work is not the whole story. That an unalienated society, or even one free of hierarchical authority, could maintain such an expansion of choices in life remains to be demonstrated. The possibility seems remote.

The Nature of Choice.—The problems raised in the discussion of these four fallacies, particularly the fourth, enable us to say something about the kinds of choices open to the individual in society as they are related to the degree of structural differentiation. It should be pointed out that mere industrialization does not mean that a society is sufficiently differentiated to warrant drawing the conclusions we are making. Totalitarian societies may be differentiated economically, but many areas of choice are restricted because of lack of differentiation of political functions from economic management, from the legal system, and from the operations of interest groups. Whatever toleration is shown to differentiated religious bodies, the Party itself is implicitly considered as the organ of both "Church" and State (cf. Aron, 1957). It is not within the scope of this book to document the ways in which American society is differentiated politically, economically, and legally so that it cannot be characterized as either a mass society in the political sense or a totalitarian society. I am, rather, concerned with confronting the ideological proposition that differentiation, or "alienation," in *any* form necessarily restricts individual freedom and that it necessarily entails the imposition of one kind of political, hierarchical authority, or that it makes people too dependent on one another. I am concerned with the implications of increased social interdependence for individual choice both as a theoretically general statement and as empirically demonstrable in American society.

In our discussion of order, we said that choice is restricted in any society in the sense that the individual cannot make any choice he wants without considering others' choices as well. At the root of this is the venerable problem that has understandably preoccupied political theory for a long time, particularly since the Enlightenment: the problem of individual liberty, or freedom, and its relation to society, or the State. For our purposes here, I will define individual freedom as the license to do anything one wants regardless of the ways in which the consequences of one's action may restrict the freedom of others. The obverse consideration is that of restricting individual freedom so that the choices of others are not curtailed. Indisputably, reconciling the two will always pose difficult problems, especially in resolving conflicts at particular levels (although the kinds of conflicts that prevail in any particular period are not the same throughout the development of a society).

We wish to summarize the implications of *structural differentiation* for freedom of individual choice and the extent to which it does or does not curtail the choices of others. In view of the preceding discussion, I suggest that it is neither a case where A necessarily gains at B's loss (the zero-sum notion of competition) nor a case where both A and B—as members of the society—relinquish choices to the State, or society, without ever gaining any new choices.

We have seen that the reformers hold this latter view with their concept of anonymous authority. This point of view is also shared by the moralizers except that they say that society, or social organization, is not something that forces individuals to give up their freedom but is something to which they abjectly relinquish their freedom.

The notion that social organization necessarily curtails freedom of choice in some area is common in many types of ideology. Perhaps it is not going too far to say that this issue—with the problem of anomie—is a central one in all ideological thinking reacting to the strains caused by structural differentiation. In an essay on C. Wright Mills' *Power Elite*, Parsons (1960) refers to this notion as individualistic utopianism and points out that, in different versions, it has characterized widely differing interpretations of modern industrial society. One such version is "Jeffersonian" liberalism with its vision of a simpler and hence "better" society as opposed to the "inhumanities and impersonalities of large-scale modern industrialism" (p. 222). The present moralizers' ideology with its humanistic emphasis, although it is not utopian, is in some ways the historical legacy on the American scene of such an approach. Another version is the "business creed" with its belief that governmental or labor-union interference is an unwarranted curtailment of businessmen's areas of choice. The same notion has characterized many versions of political theory, as in John Stuart Mill's concern with the encroachments of the State on individual liberty.

In contrast to these views, I suggest that, under favorable

conditions, members of the society may relinquish choices in one area and gain them in another. This formulation is, of course, also familiar in political theory—as, for example, in discussions of social contract. But the proposition can be stated more precisely in two directions: first, by making a qualitative distinction between what is relinquished and what is gained, and second, by making a quantitative distinction between the number of choices relinquished and the number gained.

The first proposition is that *the area of choice relinquished is of a lower order than that gained.* The individual gives up deciding what products to make or services to perform. This decision is taken over by the employing firm as a collectivity. But, with specialization, he gains freedom to choose in two respects. First, he may choose the occupational role that is suited to his particular capacities and interests and is freed from having to perform functions that others take over from him. Second, he may choose the firm in which he wants to perform that role. And he can move from firm to firm much more easily than the self-employed person can change his line of work.

Similarly, the "lack of space" in metropolitan areas and the "plenitude of the masses" of which Ortega speaks does mean that people's freedom of movement is considerably curtailed. Thus, Swados (1956) spoke of the mechanical regularity of train schedules; people are "herded about like cattle," lining up passively in queues, and the like. What he and others overlook are the cultural and occupational opportunities and the variety of experiences made available by living in metropolitan centers, advantages made possible by specialization. This is not to say that problems of demographic pressure can be dismissed on these grounds; however, for those who live in metropolitan centers, lining up in queues and obeying traffic directions can scarcely be considered a loss of freedom equivalent to the range of choices gained. In addition, those who believe that big-city life is not worth the struggle are not required to leave the small town. But the higher-level range of opportunities can not be had without foregoing the lower-level freedom of movement.

This proposition also operates on the principle that routinizing lower-level choices frees the attention for more important decisions. Often what is deplored as standardization accomplishes this very end. Many social conventions are a form of such standardization, a routinization of trivial procedures that frees people from having to solve them every time in an *ad hoc* manner. Senator Flanders states this principle in a discussion of the standardization of interchangeable parts for machinery. (I realize that an analogy with machinery will at once discredit my point in many quarters, but the principle applies as well to human behavior and the senator has expressed it very well.) He says, "We must use standards as 'the liberator' that relegates the problems that have already been solved to the field of routine and leaves the creative faculties for the problems that are still unsolved" (1951, p. 48).

The second proposition is that *the number of choices gained is greater than the number relinquished.* Two consequences of structural differentiation bring this about. First, greater specialization opens a greater range of activities—both occupational and nonoccupational—to individual participation. In a less differentiated society, the similarity of functional needs that all structures must meet is greater and the range of choices is smaller. More people do the same things. Second, differentiation increases the functional capacity of the system so that the range of choices—of available goods and services and of things to do—is greater. The rise in the gross national product is *one* aspect of such increase. As Daniel Lerner summed it up, the so-called conformist may be called a participant. "A society is participant if most people in it go through school, read newspapers, receive cash payments in jobs they are free to change, buy goods in a free market, vote in free elections, and express opinions on many matters which are not their business" (1958, p. 158).

From this point of view, we cannot unqualifiedly presume

that social organization curtails individual freedom without making the distinctions set forth by these two propositions. Moreover, structural differentiation does not simply offer individuals a wider range of opportunities from which to choose, it also may develop their potentialities as human beings and their *capacity* to make choices in terms of those potentialities. This consideration brings us to the ways in which the development of society is related to the development of the individual.

7

The Individual and Society

Up to this point, I have been using the term "individual" somewhat loosely, not wanting to seem as if I were side-stepping this ideological concern by means of some sort of jargonistic legerdemain. The way the term is used, however, tends to create confusion, as if society were something "out there" with which the "individual" is confronted. When we speak of the individual as a unique human being, the reference is to personality. (Personality, of course, involves more than uniqueness.) But this is only one aspect of individuals as concrete persons; for society as well is embodied in them and their interaction. "Society" and "personality," then, are abstractions; *both* refer at the same time to *individuals and* their *social interaction* in a cultural context. However distasteful this distinction may be to some humanists—and for many of *their* purposes it may be not necessary—it is essential if discussion hopes to be more than descriptive and not lapse into fallacies of misplaced concreteness.

Thus, personality is not an entity existing independently of society; its very nature and its degree of complexity are directly related to the complexity of society. This relationship has three aspects. The first coincides with our proposition that choices available to individuals increase with structural differentiation: there are more opportunities for individual differences to express themselves, for unique talents to find outlets. As Durkheim expressed it, "It is none the less true that individualism has developed in absolute value by penetrating into regions which were originally closed to it" (1949, p. 198). In simpler societies, the fewer opportunities for people to be different obviously means that they have to be more alike: "The more primitive societies are, the more resemblances there are among the individuals who compose them" (Durkheim, 1949, p. 133).

The second aspect is that the decline in ascription that accompanies structural differentiation means that the individual has greater freedom to pursue a range of activities (in addition to his occupation) independently of each other. The resources and the competence required for one activity are not tied to those of another from which it has been differentiated. In addition, increases in functional capacity exert a definite pressure to set aside restrictions on individual participation on the basis of ascribed characteristics such as race, religion, and sex. Whatever ascriptive barriers there are in American society—and the situation is still far from being a cause for complacency—it cannot be denied that by and large they are being lowered, whether rapidly enough or not is another question. The role of structural differentiation in this process is sometimes overlooked. Segregation, for example, is not solely a matter of moral and legal pressures and Southern attitudes; it is also subject to the pressures of a rapidly differentiating society that needs to mobilize the undeveloped resources of over 10 per cent of its members.

The third aspect of the relationship between personality and society is in line with our proposition that choices become available at higher-levels; as a consequence of this, *upgrading* occurs. The routinization of lower-level choices through social organization frees human effort for the consideration of choices requiring more intense application and the making of choices requiring greater discrimination. With the expansion of technology, human resources are also increasingly emancipated from the manipulation of things and are made available for use in their essentially human capacity—the use of the human mind.

Society—as a system of interrelationships among personalities—cannot simply be viewed as the State, as a political agency that maintains the social order and whose regulatory powers are unwillingly invoked only when necessary. *Its degree of complexity*—through structural differentiation—*emancipates personality—individuality*, if you will—*from ascriptive ties*. In less differentiated societies, personality is ascribed to a more rigid system of relationships; such rigidity is characterized not only by ascriptive ties to kinship, class, religion, location, and the like, but by a low degree of specialization as well.

Of relatively recent importance is the emancipation of personality from ascriptive ties to the family. Max Horkheimer has pointed out that bourgeois society liberated *families* rather than *individuals* from authoritarian institutions; but familial control and oppression continued, as in Victorian England with domination of woman by man and domination of children by parents—and of all by a Puritanical moral code (Dennis Wrong, 1950, p. 380). As Rabasseire, in referring to those who romanticize the family-life of the past, reminds us, "That touching picture of the happy family, gathered around the big oaken table, seems never to have been marred by the tragedies which constitute ninety per cent of the thematic material in nineteenth century literature" (1956a, p. 328).

The importance of these considerations and of their impact on personality is overlooked by the intellectuals' ideologies (and by many other ideologies as well). Their notion of the relationship of society to personality is derived from their assumptions about the nature of man. It is beyond my present purpose to trace the intellectual ancestry of these assumptions, but an examination of them in the present cases may serve to reveal what kind of implicit social theory underlies the ideology.

Assumptions about the Nature of Man

The Reformers' Version.—The reformers' ideology assumes that man is naturally good and is corrupted by social institutions. (See Judith Shklar, *After Utopia*, for example, for a discussion of the intellectual sources of this idea, particularly in nineteenth-century romanticism.) The source of the "corruption" is alienation; social institutions are seen "in the last analysis" as a structure of authority and power, of what we referred to as real factors. Economic relations are not regarded as analytically independent of that structure but are fused with it; any one particular economic relation entails one, and only one, political way of life. The independence of the legal structure in modern society is either completely shoved into the background or regarded as the tool of economic interests (Parsons, 1960, p. 219).

The importance of values and religious meanings as an aspect of culture, of ideal factors, is relegated to being considered an epiphenomenon of social institutions (authority and power). Thus, this aspect of culture is seen as "ideology" in various forms: class-consciousness, interest-seeking, and mass-opiates. Taking the place of culture is a pan-humanistic conception of man's intrinsic quality. The very meaning of man's relation to Nature, to himself, and to other men is not considered problematical in any way; it is somehow intrinsically *there* in man waiting to be released. Evil is essentially the social frustration of human nature, and the role of the intellectuals is to battle these social restraints. The social theory implicit in this point of view reduces both culture and personality to a given human nature; it reduces society to a system of power-relations. When the "favorable conditions" of man's relation to man assert themselves, utopia will be attained and power-relations will vanish. The state, for example, will wither away.

This representation of ideological assumptions perhaps seems oversimplified in that it ignores, to some extent, the many variations that have been played on the central theme of man's alienation throughout the intellectual history of this idea. These variations, however, have in common the attempt to overcome alienation by restoring to man what had been taken from him and "projected," as Daniel Bell puts it, "onto some external object or spirit" (1960, p. 339).

The differences among these variations on the theme of man's alienation lie more in the conception of what brought about the "projection," or "alienation." Thus Bell points out that for Feuerbach it was religion and for Marx it was the political economy that became the "means whereby human values are 'projected' outside of man and achieve an existence independent of him, and over him" (1960, p. 341). But both shared the notion of restoring to man what had been alienated; in other words, of eliminating the differentiation, however conceived.

Before taking up the moralizers' approach, let us first examine the elitist version, which differs from the former in certain important respects.

The Elitist Version.—As much of politically conservative thought regards man as essentially evil—or, at best, not to be trusted—and believes that he must be restrained by the State, so the elitist version of mass society and mass culture regards the mass of men as potential barbarians whose impulses and incompetence must be restrained by an elite. The elite has the special responsibility of guarding the cultural heritage and maintaining its standards. They are agents, so to speak, for that heritage. Like parents keeping order in the home, they must prevent its being demolished by children who may get out of hand. Despite various concessions to the problems of the circulation of the elite, recruitment to it is mainly on the basis of ascribed membership in the dominant social class, or through acceptance or recognition by those members, as in patronage. Any other type of social arrangement cannot be trusted as a means of recruitment, or of developing cultural potentialities among the non-elite. There is no infallible method for detecting superiority of intellect, Eliot tells us (1948, p. 102). Some mute Miltons might turn up, but with them would also appear the *Cromwells*—no longer restrained from being guiltless of their country's blood.

Under the surveillance of the dominant class (and its responsibility for high culture), culture must be borne, according to Eliot, by a gradation of classes; its transmission requires the persistence of classes and regional diversity (1948, p. 15). Culture, then, is ascribed to class and region. The social theory implicit in this point of view sees society as a stable (relatively rigid) class structure to which both culture and personality are ascribed. Insofar as the nature of man is concerned, his potential evil is to be restrained by class definition and class barriers. His potential good is his responsibility to live up (or down) to the station in which he is born.

Those who are not of the dominant class and yet ascend to the cultural elite are the exception to such ascription. Their ability to transcend the status of their birth seems to be regarded as innate: geniuses are born, not made *or* developed. *Real* Miltons would not remain mute. The human potentialities that the reformers see as universally given and waiting to spring into frondescence with the removal of social restraints are here regarded as sparingly granted to the few "great men" who will assert them in spite of restraints.

It should be pointed out at this time that, insofar as American society is concerned, the elitists' version represents a deviation from the basic values of the society in a way that the moralizers' and the reformers' versions do not. The notion of an established aristocratic elite and a relatively rigid class structure contradicts the American valuation of equality of opportunity and of freedom for the individual to choose his own goals in life. Neither Ortega nor Eliot, of course, presume to speak for American society. But those who adopt *this* point of view when referring to mass culture in American society seem to be suggesting that the standards that apply to "cultural" activities should somehow be sealed off from the more general values.

Since these assumptions about man and his place in society affect the shape that an ideological formulation takes on, it is analytically important to trace their relation to basic religious and ontological premises. This relationship between ideology and religion is, it seems to me, more than a mere analogy, or a mere borrowing of one scheme of thought from another already available. I regard assumptions about the nature of man and of his life in society as *derived from* such a grounding of meaning. As derivations, they, too, go through an "evolutionary process," through stages of reinterpretation.

The thought structure of the elitist version of society has certain resemblances with that of medieval Roman Catholicism. The hierarchical ordering of supernature and nature is reflected in the stable class structure. The distinction between what is expected from those in orders and from the laity resembles the distinction between the elite and the non-elite. The ability of those in orders to lay up a surplus of grace for the benefit of the laity has its equivalence in the notion that the elite is the principal guardian, creator, and transmittor of culture for the rest of the society. Eliot is perhaps referring to this same resemblance when he says, ". . . the convert of the intellectual or sensitive type [the elitist type] is drawn towards the more Catholic type of worship and doctrine. . . . It is always the main religious body which is the guardian of more of the remains of the higher developments of culture preserved from a past time . . ." (1948, p. 80).

The Moralizers' Version.—In our discussion of mass culture, we subsumed the elitist version under the value-orientation because in both cases, the focus was on maintaining values instead of on unfavorable social conditions; similarly, both have a humanistic emphasis. There are, however, important differences in their assumptions. From the moralizers' point of view, the ascription of the individual to class is either denied or not overtly admitted. There is a belief in the dignity of every man as an individual endowed with free will and a belief in the power of human reason. But these cannot be taken for granted as intrinsic in human nature. They are ideals in a cultural heritage that must be continually preserved and transmitted through education, exhortation, and criticism. The responsibility for this preservation and transmission falls on the intellectuals; the responsibility of individuals is to affirm these ideals, to assert their own freedom and humanity.

The present state of affairs is blamed on the defection of the individual; the only cure for current troubles is the individual's will to reassert what he has abandoned. The nature of man is assumed, then, to be potentially good *or* evil. In certain explicit formulations (e.g., Corliss Lamont, *Humanism as a Philosophy*), the humanistic point of view is avowedly secular and repudiates any supernatural legitimation. Where this is not the case, there tends to be an attraction to denominations (e.g., Unitarian) and beliefs (e.g., Tillich existentialism) where the theological framework is broad enough for humanistic latitudinarianism.

It is, however, of some interest to point out certain resemblances between the moralizers' beliefs about man and Arminian theology, a religious orientation that underlies much of American Protestantism. This comparison is by no means intended as a parody; it is drawn to show an important relationship between these current beliefs and a religious basis (as in the previous case) that, I believe, has influenced its formulation. Given the assumption about the individual's capacity both to fall by the wayside and to pull himself back into line, this point of view, like the Arminian position, sees the "state of grace" as conditional. Universal redemption is available for all in cultural ideals; atonement has been made by "the ideals of the best minds, the saving remnant of the human race" (see the Bush quotation on page 27). But only believers will partake of the benefit. Man, in order to maintain faith (his cultural commitments), must be regenerated and renewed by the humanities and their agents, the intellectuals.

The difference between the assumptions made by this point of view and those made by the elitist version of the nature of man reflect the change that was brought about by the Reformation. In the Roman Catholic case, individuals were either in orders or of the laity; different religious expectations applied to each. With the Reformation, however, this separate allocation was effaced and the same religious criteria applied to all (Troeltsch, 1931). As Weber, following Sebastian Franck's formulation, expressed it: ". . . every Christian had to be a monk all his life" (1958, p. 121). Although man retained his secular role as well, what was expected of him in the religious sense became his individual responsibility; his dependence on the Church and on those in orders—and his *ascription* to them—was broken. To that degree, his state of grace became more problematical and he could more easily fall by the wayside. There was—if you will—an upgrading of religious expectations.

Similarly, the moralizers' assumptions have effaced the elitists' distinction between elite and non-elite. Cultural expectations—awareness of them and commitment to them —apply to all men. Everyone is expected to become a member of the "elite"; failure to do so is a form of backsliding, a fall from grace—evident in the "spiritual flabbiness" of our time, as President Kirk of Columbia University has called it.

With regard to the social theory implicit in this point of view, the moralizers might justifiably deny any intention (much less any inclination!) of stating one at all. But since they are analyzing the individual in a social context (however undesirable the latter may be), some notion of the relevance of this context must be put into perspective. They focus on culture and personality, but within certain limited aspects of them. They emphasize the moral aspects of culture—particularly individual freedom of thought and the forces of individual will and reason. These are the most precious and hard-won fruits of a cultural heritage whose record of human virtue and folly can heighten man's awareness of his own experience and invest it with meaning.

But they scarcely recognize social organization as having any part in the picture. Desirable social arrangements, like the legal process, the protection of human rights, education, etc., tend to be treated solely as epiphenomena of cultural ideals. The rest is regarded as an unfortunately necessary means of regulation in an imperfect world—or, when social organization goes too far, as downright undesirable and something to be resisted. With their deemphasis of social organization, the moralizers unwittingly emphasize the way in which all individuals are *alike*: all men have a personal responsibility to society as a moral community. But the moralizers often fail to see that the very complexity of social organization that they deplore increases the number of different ways in which individuals may fulfill that responsibility. They also fail to see that increasing structural differentiation raises the level of that responsibility for a larger proportion of people in the society.

While the moralizers see individuals as bound together by cultural ideals, they consider society itself as an aggregate of its individual members; it can be nothing more or less than the sum of them. "In the last analysis," they seem to imply, individuals acting independently of each other are the society's only resource. As in a "great-man" theory of history, individual greatness alone makes worthwhile contributions and individual corruption alone portends the moral disintegration of the larger community. One bad apple spoils the barrel. The way in which social organization makes individual contributions possible is not only shoved into the background, it is dismissed as "false collectivization" (Whyte, 1956, p. 55) or by the conceptual trick of reifying society and then pointing out the fallacy of reification. According to a review of MacLeish's television drama *The Secret of Freedom* (Lottman, 1960), one of the characters, an ancient librarian, tells us that "nations don't dream, men dream."

Even though the moralizers deemphasize the importance of society, they do make a differentiation with respect to culture that the reformers do not. A comparison between the two may now be drawn. The aspect of culture of particular relevance here is the way in which it provides evaluative, or moral, standards in terms of which human action may be judged. The reformers believe these standards can be derived from the study of man himself; they reside in a pan-humanistic conception of the nature of man and are therefore an *immanent* reference. The values that have been "projected" outside of man, as Bell put it, are to be "put back into man"; instead of being independent of him, they will be inherent in him.

The moralizers' version, however, does not believe man's nature is intrinsically good and that moral standards can be derived from it alone. On the contrary, man's action is to be judged against such standards as a *transcendent* reference. In this sense, the moralizers' assumptions are *more differentiated;* culture is an analytically independent reference, not reduced to and derived from conceptions of "human nature." It provides an additional reference point from which human action may be appraised. It furnishes a leverage for upgrading what is expected of human action and therefore does not assume that the nature of what that action should be is already defined, or implicit.

The reformers do away with the possibility of such leverage by not making that differentiation. With their immanent reference, no standards can be set up apart from human action since they are derived from its "intrinsic" nature to begin with. Everything is reduced to a romantic version of human nature and any moral basis of action—such as religion—is not distinct from man but is inherent in him. There is no carrot to hold in front of the donkey.

Society: Between Culture and Personality

As an alternative to the above notions about the nature of man and his relation to society, I want to carry further my previous comments about the implications that increasing social complexity has for personality and—in consequence—bring into the picture a different conception of society. To recapitulate, we have seen how structural differentiation increases opportunities for individual differences, reduces ascription, and increases the range of choices at more significantly human levels through increases in functional capacity and upgrading.

It is by now quite clear that, according to the point of view being developed here, it is not considered very useful to talk about the "nature of man" independently of the social and cultural context he lives in, unless by "man" one means culture, society, personality, and biological organism taken together as represented in any concrete person. This position is not meant to imply a complete cultural and sociological relativism about man's nature, but it is meant to examine how far one can go in specifying it without falling into what I consider to be misleading assumptions.

As an alternative to some of the assumptions we have reviewed, I would like to speak first of the nature of *personality* —perhaps a somewhat chilling and less grand concept than that of "man," but one that gives us a point of departure that leads, in my opinion, to less chilling conclusions about the potentialities for man's life in modern society.

The Development of Personality.—For the sake of simplicity, we have referred to personality as that aspect of man which refers to his uniqueness as a human being, that which differentiates him from all others. We have then said that society, through structural differentiation, emancipates that personality from ascriptive ties. Emancipation, however, does not just *release* uniqueness as something completely "given" in every individual regardless of the society he lives in; it helps to *create* it by developing the personality itself to higher levels of complexity and greater potentiality.

As the personality plays an increasing number of roles in a greater variety of differentiated situations, he has to discriminate among them, among the varying kinds of relationships he has with other people. Greater demands, moreover, are made on him through the process of upgrading. If he made no discriminations from one situation to another— whether the situation be family, work, play, or whatever— meaningful human relationships would obviously collapse. For this reason, the personality does not relate to others in an *ad hoc* manner—playing every situation by ear, so to speak; nor does his behavior result solely from his "thinking for himself." He knows to some extent what is expected of him and what he expects of others in terms of generalized patterns of behavior, or norms, that define the situation for him. These generalized patterns of relating to others become part of his personality structure. This is an oversimplified statement of what Parsons (1958) means when he says that the ego-structure of the personality consists in internalized social-object systems, a formulation based on an interpretation of Freud's *The Ego and the Id.*

In addition, the crucial importance of culture in this development cannot be overlooked, although the ideological issues we are confronting do not require that we examine in detail its relation to personality. As a statement in the form of a paraleipsis, the personality not only draws from the available cultural heritage by learning a body of knowledge, he also internalizes standards of behavior that the culture embodies—moral, esthetic, and cognitive discriminations.

Culture is here considered to be analytically independent of society. As a determinant of behavior, culture is a pattern of *meanings*—of the meaning of social and physical reality to human action; it is on the basis of culture that discriminations are made. Society, on the other hand, is a pattern of human relationships which culture makes meaningful and within which cultural discriminations are made (see Kroeber and Parsons, 1958). In passing, it may be pointed out that society facilitates the development of culture as well as that of personality through such social arrangements as education, research, and the like. These social arrangements are by no means a mere emanation of cultural patterns.

Thus, with the increasing complexity both of the cultural heritage and of social interaction, the personality becomes more highly organized. Structural differentiation in both culture and society means structural differentiation in the personality; categories of discrimination and patterns of role-relationships become internalized at increasingly higher levels of organization. Thus, with the evolution of more complex cultural and social systems, the personality of man is also continuing to go through a process of evolution—not just in the ontogenetic sense (as in the development of the individual) but in the phylogenetic sense (as in the development from generation to generation).

The uniqueness of personality, or individuality, comes not from simply presenting a *given* unique entity with a range of choices for self-expression to which it "responds" in the manner of someone passing through a cafeteria line; nor do these choices "condition" it, like Pavlov's dog. In fact, choices *and* the standards for making them become a structurally organized part of the personality; they become internalized.

From this point of view, the only thing that can be mentioned about the nature of man *apart* from the social and cultural components of such nature is the genetic constitution with which he is born. Although the genetic constitution is a crucial determinant, it is here regarded as a *nonspecific* base; an infant can learn any language or internalize any general cultural pattern; the *patterns* internalized are not determined by the genes, whatever limitations the genes place on his capacity. Thus advanced cultures will contain certain components so difficult to understand—such as, say, higher mathematics—that not every person will have the capacity to make them his own. This quality of nonspecificity is often referred to as the plasticity of the human organism and is reflected in Freud's notion that the infant is polymorph perverse.

For these reasons, I question the inferences Fromm draws from his assumption that human nature has an *intrinsic* quality of its own independent of what society and culture do with it. He explicitly states that man's potentialities are "prepared in the present . . . the future stage of development can be described by saying that the future virtually exists in the present" (1947, p. 217). His analogy with the tree is revealing, for man similarly is alleged to unfold under favorable "conditions." Fromm states that man is endowed with the capacity of speaking (1947, p. 217) and that if it is blocked, he is severely damaged [as in the cases of feral children]. This capacity may very well be intrinsic, but learning a language is not simply a matter of conditioning, or of learning words and how to speak them intelligibly. It is— among other things—internalizing what linguists call a *code* which not only orders the words but also orders the references to what is being talked about. And since what is internalized varies from language to language, it seems more fruitful to regard this as a significant addition to the personality rather than as the unfolding of a capacity.

It is on the basis of Fromm's assumption of an intrinsic human nature that he and others who share it say they can tell us what man "really" wants, or "ought" to want—such as deciding what products to make, wanting to be close to Nature, wanting to participate in overall management of work-processes. Substitute the words "specifically determined" for "intrinsic" and then one can proceed to prescribe specific social arrangements. It is premature—and probably always will be—to *specify* what man wants. As Lovell Thompson says, ". . . we should speak of lost needs rather than lost desires" (1951, p. 57). Statements about what man "needs" or "wants" are more wisely made in general terms, such as Freud's *lieben und arbeiten* (love and work).

Despite the fact that the reformers take a rather specific view of what "desirable" social conditions are supposed to be, they are at least aware of the fact that the development of personality is not as independent of society as the moralizers seem to suggest. The ability of man to perceive alternatives and to make choices is more than simply a matter of "standing on his own feet" and "thinking for himself"—particularly in a democratic society, I would add. Moral exhortation alone cannot instill in man the requisite commitment to values or the motivation to develop his capacities if the social context he lives in has not yet made them a part of his personality. The moralizers are partially aware of these problems in their justifiable concern over the need for more or better education, although I suspect that educational resources are often deemed desirable because they are viewed as an extension of humanistic exhortation. We are familiar enough with their reservations about "too much science" (not to mention that *bête noire*, behavioral science).

Moralizers tend to view society as the consequence of individual actions. Concretely, this is, of course, obvious. *Man* writes laws, editorials, and speeches; *man* takes action and asserts leadership. But he does not do so on the sole basis of God-given or humanistically inspired individuality; he does so in the context of a society whose very complexity enhances and necessitates the assertion of individuality. Indeed, from the standpoint of upgrading, social complexity forces the development of his potentialities. A balanced account of the situation cannot be given without considering the social framework in which concrete individual acts take place. Legal institutions, voluntary associations, and the much maligned "groupism" are structural features of the society that make individual moral action something more than random heroism. They not only channel individual action but partly generate it as well. They organize human effort in such a way that old problems do not have to be faced anew every time they arise and new problems have some established reference from which to proceed.

Such organization forces the individual to come to terms with the conditions of social interaction. As discussed in Chapter 1, patterns of interaction among persons have to be worked out; they cannot simply emanate from values, individual will, or good intentions. If the cultural heritage depended on nothing but individual dedication, then indeed "democracy would have to be reinvented with each generation," as MacLeish's librarian is reported to have said (Lottman, 1960). The cultural heritage is safeguarded and preserved not only by elites or by individuals but *by social organization* as well. By the latter, I do not simply mean law courts and civic groups and the like; I mean social organization in its broadest sense, including other-directed peer-groups and committee meetings.

Intermediate Structures in Society.—Of crucial importance in such organization are the associations—the human groups —that lie *between* the intimate relations among family and friends and the more extensive bureaucratic organization of big government and big business. Kornhauser, among others (Tocqueville, for instance, was exceptionally acute about this problem), has emphasized the importance of these structures and refers to them as "intermediate relations":

These intermediate relations function as links between the individual and his primary relations, on the one hand, and the state and other national relations, on the other hand. It must be emphasized that voluntary associations are not the only kind of intermediate relation; all organized relations that mediate between the family and the nation, such as the local government and the local press, are classified as intermediate structures. . . . (1959, p. 74)

Kornhauser points out how such groups "look both ways." In one direction, they represent the interests of particular groups—labor, professions, parents, those concerned with cultural or political activities—vis-à-vis the larger community. And they protect those interests from being crushed or passed over by a public unsympathetic or even unacquainted with their needs. They make individual action possible through participation and give the individual a sense of control.

In the other direction, they insulate the larger society from irresponsible mass action. In facing the increasingly complex issues that arise in modern society, individual responsibility cannot be taken for granted. This is not to say, in elitist fashion, simply that the individual cannot be trusted without social restraints, but that individual capacities *and* competence vary. This is particularly true of competence from one area of interest to another. It is not simply a question of social restraints but of social organization that recruits competence for leadership (and specialized competence for the interest at hand) and a followership by eliciting individual commitments and a sense of responsibility.

There seems to be evidence that leaders of groups and organizations are likely to be the more responsible (better educated and more libertarian) members of the community (Kornhauser, 1959, pp. 56-72 and Stouffer, 1955). Kornhauser's data also shows that group-members—Daniel Lerner's "participants"—have more interest in political affairs, are more likely to be better informed and to be nonauthoritarian.

Conversely, Lipset shows that "non-participants"—those who are *"isolated* from the activities, controversies, and organizations of democratic society" are prevented "from acquiring the sophisticated and complex view of the political structure which makes understandable and necessary the norms of tolerance" (1960, p. 112). As Kornhauser puts it:

Non-participation results in lack of exposure to information and indoctrination concerning democratic values, and in the lack of habits of discussion, debate, negotiation, and compromise—modes of conduct indispensable to democratic politics. (1959, p. 73)

With specialization, intermediate groups are concerned with "only limited aspects of [their] members' lives" (p. 78). Religion comes to be separated from politics, and education, from trade, for example. This means that individual contributions to one sphere can be made independently of those to another, that the claims of each interest to the resources of society can be formulated more clearly, and that strain in any one part of the system is less likely to spread to other parts of the society. In a less differentiated type of society, a disturbance in the performance of one function affects all other functions to which it is structurally ascribed.

Moreover, there is a pluralism of affiliations in that there are different combinations of members in each group. Kornhauser points out that associations have members with a variety of class and ethnic identities, occupational roles and religious affiliations. Such pluralism makes for cross-cutting solidarities that restrain ideological polarization and what Kornhauser more inclusively calls social cleavage.

Individual commitments to values and individual independence in expressing opinions are, of course, essential contributions to social effort; social organization is not in itself a sufficient resource. But its importance not only for providing the framework for recruiting individual action but for informing it and generating it cannot be dismissed as "togetherness," or as an anonymous-authority structure. The absence of such intermediate relations does indeed characterize a mass society where a non-participant and unengaged public is prey to demagogic appeal. Commitment to principles of individual freedom and morality, however inspiring, require specification before they may be implemented in action. Organization of social interaction defines purposes and allocates responsibility. One wonders just what it is the individual is expected to do after being exhorted to think for himself and to resist conforming. There are several steps to be taken between reaffirming spiritual values and getting school bond issues passed.

It is by means of such group-affiliation that the individual overcomes his "atomized" isolation and powerlessness. Participation in collective effort restores to him a measure of control —in labor unions, over his work processes; in professional and trade associations, over the standards of his occupation; in PTA, over the education of his children. It is through such means, that "the area of personal and social control" may be increased, that the "responsible determination of one's personal life may perhaps be linked with responsible co-determination in public life." These are Lewis Coser's words (1956b, p. 163). They define what he considers the central issue in our society today. I could not agree more, although the article from which these words are taken suggests that he would quite likely describe my point of view as a defense of the *status quo*. (The level at which one defines *status quo* in a rapidly changing society is of some relevance here.)

Some Comments on "Organization Man."—We have already discussed the impact of specialization on bureaucratic organization and pointed out how it tends to break down the old-style pattern of line authority and not only allows but necessitates participation by more people in decision-making processes. The control over the situation is allocated among persons in terms of specialized competence. One might argue that this measure of control represents a limited range of choice insofar as "running the business" is concerned, but such an argument may be using the wrong frame of reference. That is, the specialist may view *his* involvement in his work and the range of choices open to him more in terms of the universalistic standards of his specialized knowledge rather than in terms of over-all control of the organization he works for.

The only other alternatives to this arrangement are the moralizers' implication that power be returned to the so-called inner-directed rugged individualist, who "thinks for himself" instead of worrying about what everyone else is thinking, or the reformers' recommendation of establishing joint participation by all in all capacities, on the basis of the romanticized small-town meeting. The moralizers' course divests everyone except the boss of the right to participate in decision-making (although the implication is, ideally, that everyone is a boss). The reformers' course would drastically reduce effectiveness in large groups or require that all organization be on a small scale—an impossibility in many industries, not to mention government. It is indisputable that complex decisions can only be formulated by small groups, as the committee-system in Congress illustrates.

In the "unalienated" society, as suggested by Fromm's communitarian socialism, responsibilities would be allocated among groups of persons as well, the allocation being a community decision. The main difference between such an arrangement and that in an "alienated" society seems to be that recruitment in the "unalienated" case would not be on the basis of specialized (hence alienated) competence but on the basis of particularistic community ties. (One is reminded of Mary McCarthy's *The Oasis*.) We are entitled to question how effective such an arrangement would be in securing either social justice or in getting things done. Any advantage in one area of decision yields advantage in many; any disturbance in one area quickly spreads to all.

Beyond these considerations lies the issue of collaborative work among specialists themselves or among those in closely related fields. In attacking this form of participation as togetherness, the intellectuals are overlooking what Harry Stack Sullivan referred to as consensual validation. Very few individual thinkers are infallible; in presenting their ideas before others, they can test them for weaknesses and oversights. Others often fill in gaps and correct errors; they stimulate the individual thinker and enable him to break through difficulties. Whyte's comment that "people rarely *think* in groups" is sheer distortion of the facts.

In the academic context, it is perhaps the case that scientific work benefits from these procedures more than work in the humanities. Scientific standards of investigation and of proof are more universal criteria of appraisal than those applied to the humanities, which are more particularistic in their approach.

The point being made here is that work in groups is often both necessary and constructive; it does not mean to imply that group-work solves all problems. No amount of "group-think" will provide a substitute for individual effort and it is obvious that little can be got out of people who have not done their homework before they go to a meeting. The intellectuals quite correctly warn us of what is undoubtedly a tendency in many quarters to believe that throwing everyone together in a room will generate creative thought.

Any social resource, however, is subject to misuse. The question is not an either-or proposition: either it works all the time or it should be thrown out. Man did not discard the use of fire because it burned him. It is a question of the extent to which it may be utilized to contribute to human effort. Nor does a Gresham's law operate indefinitely, in the sense that the allegedly easier way out ("group-think") drives out the use of "better" resources (individual thinking). Not only evaluative standards but the pressure to attain desirable ends places a check on abuses running rampant indefinitely. The intellectual exhortations—exaggerated though they are—are a valuable reminder of these standards.

The animadversion on working-in-groups is also related to the larger question of the manipulation of human beings—not only in groups but through mass media, as in advertising, public relations, and the like. Intellectuals frequently point out that certain businessmen and "Madison-Avenue types," eager to exploit the potentialities of social scientific techniques, will turn them to their advantage without respect for human rights. In the first place, there is considerable fantasy —both on the part of those alarmed *and* of the reputed exploiters—as to the effectiveness of such techniques. (Insofar as the present *state of knowledge* is concerned, those in the behavioral sciences would be gratified to know as much as they are credited with.) Even if such fantasies became justified, however, there is no reason to assume—again, as in Gresham's law—that there are no institutional restraints on such abuse.

The recent investigation of advertising techniques and of mass communication in general indicates that ethical standards are being sought with every possibility of their being established. Standards in this area have been uncertain for some time; a state of anomie has prevailed. It has been assumed, in *many* quarters, that "pitch-man" techniques in selling and entertainment were to be taken for granted and generally accepted. What is now seen as the revelation of gross immorality may very well be the judgment of old practices in terms of higher standards. Morality has been "upgraded" and applied to new areas of social interaction. It is a phenomenon familiar to sociology that the upgrading of standards results in what is called *relative deprivation*. That is to say, the discrepancy between what is going on and what is considered desirable becomes relatively greater when standards of desirability are raised. Thus, increased immorality is not necessarily an increase in immoral practices but rather a rise in the standards applied to the same old practices.

The relation of relative deprivation to ideology as a form of social criticism is extremely important and should be clarified in order to avoid the implication that ideology is a bad thing just because it is scientifically incorrect. Ideological criticism of the way things are is both justifiable and desirable in that it tries to improve the existing state of affairs, to close the gap between it and the way things ought to be. Standards of the way things ought to be, however, are continually being raised, or upgraded. We expect life to deliver more than we used to, whether we realize it or not. Whenever standards rise at any given time, the actual state of affairs then seems worse than before even though it has remained the same— hence, *relative* deprivation.

Indeed, often as the state of affairs improves, the improvement itself causes standards of expectations to rise even *more* rapidly so that the gap between the desirable and the actual is widened. When the newly improved conditions are then judged by the new standards, they seem worse than what preceded them. When a man's income, for example, jumps from $5,000 to $10,000 a year, the new possibility of his making even more money may cause him to be more dissatisfied at the $10,000 level than he was at the old $5,000 level.

Much of social criticism stems from the same phenomenon. As improvements in man's lot are realized, the possibility of further improvements causes expectations to rise even more rapidly. Naturally, these expectations exert pressure for additional changes and may have desirable consequences. But in assessing the *actual* state of affairs, ideological critics do so relatively—in terms of the new and higher standards as if they had always prevailed. Consequently they describe contemporary empirical conditions as having become worse.

However effective in improving conditions such criticism may be, it does not give an empirically accurate description of what is happening in the society and of what the current state of affairs actually is. In the first instance, then, I am not denying the right of ideologists to attempt to improve society. I am saying that their empirical description of society cannot be regarded as sociologically reliable. Beyond this, however, I am also saying that empirically accurate description is not the only issue at stake. Misinterpretations of the way in which society works may stem from sources other than relative deprivation. They also stem from selective biases in various kinds of social theory that fail to take into account all of the necessary factors, as we have seen. And these biases, no matter how well-intentioned the criticism that takes its departure from them, are not always helpful in clarifying issues and enabling us to face them realistically.

The Implications for Cultural Development.—I have suggested that society, by means of more complex organization, can make the link between personality and cultural standards more flexible. In less differentiated societies, the tie between cultural prescriptions and the way in which they determine individual action is more rigid. The greater the degree of ascription in any given society, the more this tie approaches a one-to-one relationship. Social complexity, however, increases the number of ways in which individual actions may be organized to attain what is considered culturally desirable. We have focussed on the implications that this has for greater freedom of individual choice, but it should be pointed out that social organization has a positive consequence for culture as well as for personality.

Through the increased flexibility that results from social complexity and differentiation, the conception of what are considered desirable cultural standards continues to advance beyond what is attainable at any given time as new ranges of choice at higher levels are opened up. There is nothing mystical intended by this suggestion; it is not as if man were trying to reach an unattainable perfection that eludes his grasp, like the donkey chasing the carrot. Although I would not quarrel with such a notion, the phenomenon can also be explained simply by the fact that answers to old questions give rise to new questions.

Any level of organization of human action that "solves," or routinizes, old problems in itself raises problems of a higher order that remain to be solved. Modern society may have solved the problem of subsistence, but a primitive society would not face the problem this book confronts. This phenomenon is inherent in the process of evolution with its successive stages of development. Utopia is not attained by arresting the process at any given point along the way. At any stage of development, two alternatives seem to present themselves: 1) enduring present problems and leaving them unsolved, or 2) solving them and thereby creating new problems of a different order. The essential point is that an evolutionary process advances by qualitatively different states, each with a level of organization that poses problems of its own. It is not a "unilinear advance" that simply reduces a *fixed quantity* of problems *given* at the start. This point is by no means news to the physical sciences, but it cannot be said to be common knowledge among those who analyze society.

8

Interpretation of Current Strain

We have seen that social change that increases the complexity of social organization—structural differentiation—also increases the range of choices available to individuals in society. Differentiation enables these choices to be made more and more independently of one another; ascription declines. The ways in which one kind of choice is tied to another because both are embedded in the same structural part of the society come to be reduced.

With this greater flexibility, the society and those in it are able to do things more effectively and can do more kinds of things; functional capacity increases. We sorted out two aspects of this consequence. The first is a horizontal aspect, extensity, wherein increasingly large proportions of the population get caught up in the ensuing changes and their consequences. The second is a vertical aspect, upgrading, wherein both levels of performance and expectations of that performance rise. That is to say, the increase in performance that results from greater functional capacity leads in turn to even higher levels of expectation or standards of what ought to be done. And, finally, the resulting discrepancy between expectations and actuality, newly defined at these higher levels, creates relative deprivation, itself giving added impetus to the upgrading effected by differentiation in the first place.

Since our ideological concern is with the individual and society, we are particularly interested in the impact of this upgrading on individuals, in the greater demands made on them. Durkheim was aware of this upgrading when he noted that through the division of labor, or structural differentiation, individuals face demands for "greater specialization, harder work, and intensification of their faculties" (1949, pp. 336-37).

The Source of Strain

It is a central point of this book that the strain to which the intellectual ideologies are reacting arises from *the greater demands for personality development.* Greater demands are being made on individuals to achieve higher levels of performance, and this performance is of a qualitatively different type than that which our past experience has led us to expect. The most important shift is from working with things to *working with people.* There are two features to this shift. The first is the *expansion of technology* that has reduced the extent to which human resources are applied to working with things with the consequence that they are made available for action of a more completely human character.

The second is *functional specialization* with the consequence that individual contributions have to be increasingly co-ordinated with each other. Co-ordination of human effort raises additional problems in that human beings do not confront one another solely with respect to getting things done. Individual likes and dislikes, prejudices, emotional needs to be liked and approved, or to be domineering or submissive inevitably intrude. Although they may not be relevant to accomplishing the task at hand, they must be taken into account if the human resources are to be utilized at all. In addition, greater demands for performance *intensify* the problem of handling emotional needs. Therefore, as individual personalities play increasingly specialized roles in social interaction, the problem of personality-management becomes increasingly salient. There is the problem of maintaining a balance between demands for performance and the need for emotional support. The individual must not only manage his *own* personality vis-à-vis others; he must be sensitive to the fact that *others* have the same problem as well.

Moreover, because of structural differentiation in the society, each individual himself plays an increasing number and variety of roles. This entails a higher level of organization in the personality; the individual must internalize a wider range of different sets of norms that define behavior in different relational contexts. As personality becomes more differentiated, the individual must *integrate* the larger number of roles he plays in order to maintain his identity—"the ability to experience one's self as something that has continuity" (Erikson, 1950, p. 38).

The individual can no longer be guided by the same established patterns of behavior that characterized a more highly ascribed society. He no longer, for example, simply follows in his father's footsteps, or stays in his "class" or even in the community he grew up in. Indeed, the very emancipation of personality from ascribed ties enables it to become a more fluid resource—not only for the society but for the individual as well. What he loses in (ascribed) certainty, he gains in flexibility. Erikson was very much aware of this problem when he said, "And so it comes about that we begin to conceptualize matters of identity at the very time in history when they become a problem" (1950, p. 242).

As Dennis Wrong points out in his discussion of the family, this reduction in ascribed guides to behavior undoubtedly creates uncertainty in courtship, in marriage, and in child-rearing with all the possibilities for anomic disturbances—to which may be added, for our purposes, uncertainty in occupational choice. But, as Wrong adds, it also creates an "inevitable expansion of the area of the personal freedom of the individual [italics omitted]. . . . This is more difficult, emotionally, and creates a confused situation socially and morally: but what else can freedom mean?" (1950, p. 380).

This freedom *does* mean an upgrading of demands on personality of yet a different kind than that required by increasing specialization. It means an upgrading of the individual's ability to explore and to choose for himself. Indeed, with the decline in ascription, he is forced to do so. Concomitant with the increased necessity of social interaction, lack of ascription requires an increasing consciousness of personality problems—both of one's own and of others. It requires, as Lipset points out, the ability to take a complex view and abstract from concrete experience; it requires imagination (1960, p. 115).

To summarize, the current strain arises from greater demands for personality development within which we can specify four problems in the two broad areas of upgrading and integration:

1) Upgrading the level of performance in particular areas
2) Upgrading the consciousness of and understanding of human relations
    —of personality problems
    —of social complexity
3) Integrating the personality: the problem of identity
4) Integrating motivational resources: maintaining the balance between demands for performance and the need for emotional support.

Upgrading and integration can be directly related to our two propositions about the impact of structural differentiation on the nature of choice. Upgrading is the consequence of the routinization of choices at lower levels and of the facing of new ones at higher levels; integration is the consequence of the fact that the number and variety of choices at higher levels are greater than those relinquished at lower levels.

Regression as a Reaction to Strain

A common reaction to the strain that results from differentiation is the desire (explicit or implicit) to return to a less differentiated stage when the problems presented by the newly emerging level of organization did not exist. This sort of reaction is called *regression*. Although Chapter 9 deals specifically with the ideological reactions to the current strain and the ways in which those reactions may be said to be forms of regression, a few more general comments may perhaps be made at this time.

Regression is related to the strains of upgrading and integration in that it emphasizes what is lost (the negative side) and ignores what is gained (the positive side). We have seen how differentiation necessitates making increasing distinctions and integrating them so that a meaningful relationship among parts on the new level can be established. One regressive reaction to this integrative problem is to throw the whole thing up as a bad job and claim that integration is not possible. This reaction is the one we are familiar with as the claim of *alienation*. It also tends to ignore the increased range of choices available at new levels and to focus on the *loss of choices* at lower levels (as in man's freedom to make work-choices).

Such regression is often justified by a romanticizing of the past as a time when "more choice" and "less alienation" prevailed. In addition, the problems that such a less differentiated past presented and that have now been solved are usually played down or ignored. If they are recognized at all, it is assumed that we can retain the solutions that our *present* level of organization has made possible and at the same time return to a simpler level.

Mrs. Shklar describes this desire to return to the past as a "cultural longing" characteristic of romanticism. "It was a yearning for Greece, first, then for the world of Ossian and for the colorful Middle Ages, and later for the Renaissance as well—indeed for any time more blessed than the present" (1957, p. 16). Thus, the medieval craftsman is idealized, for his work was not alienated from his art. The gargoyles on cathedrals are evidence of the spontaneous artistic expression of the worker. The pre-modern peasant community is idealized as one in which all men felt themselves to be integral parts of a meaningful whole. But the disease and poverty, the social injustices and superstition, the illiteracy and ignorance—they are either not mentioned or assumed to be preferable to contemporary evils.

But any reference to the past—be it to the Middle Ages or to classical antiquity—must be put into the perspective of man's entire development. Without such perspective, the vantage point in the present from which a particular assessment of the past is made will tend to focus on a few highly selected aspects of certain past eras that seem to have provided what the present era lacks. Historical judgment succumbs to the current ideology and the empirical delineation of the past becomes distorted when it is seen through the lens of contemporary problems.

The entire history of mankind may be seen as a record of evolutionary stages at all levels—cultural, social, and psychological—and the progression from one stage to another has inevitably involved profound disturbances. When Neolithic man—who domesticated plants and animals—first planted seeds, he had to forego the freedom to move about as he pleased and he had to make a future commitment to be on the same spot for the harvest. But in so doing he augmented his food supply (Childe, 1954, p. 48).

During the Copper Age, metallurgists were, according to Childe, the first "specialists," because their craft was more difficult and was not divulged to all members of the community. The occupations of mining, smelting, and casting were full-time jobs and were "the first industries not normally conducted within the household to provide for domestic needs, but to meet the demands of others. The operators [had to] rely for their sustenance mainly on surplus foodstuffs produced by their customers" (1954, p. 78). Relative to the social arrangements existing at that time, they were more drastically "alienated" than the nineteenth-century millhand. Before that time, there was probably no division of labor except that between the sexes. Only when Neolithic

farmers produced surpluses above their own requirements
(another future commitment) and when these surpluses became available to support new economic classes not directly
engaged in producing their own food could mankind overcome the limitations of the Neolithic period. The production
of surpluses in company with spectacular advances in applied
science (about 4,000-3,000 B.C.) made possible the economic
reorganization of society that Childe calls the urban revolution.

I have made this brief reference to the early development
of man to dramatize the structural similarity with the problems of differentiation we face now—the foregoing of choices
on one level, the making of future commitments, the demands for higher levels of performance, and the ensuing
reorganization. One can well imagine the resistance there
was to such changes in prehistoric times.

The structural differentiation in society that Childe dates
from the Copper Age and that has proceeded with mounting
complexity ever since has been accompanied by an evolution
of the personality structure as well, but perhaps not until
very recent times—perhaps since the Second World War in
American society—has personality been emancipated from
ascription to at least *some* part of the society—whether it
be caste, class, or even family—for any significant portion of
the population.

The upshot of these changes is that each stage has en-
tailed increasing differentiation, or alienation, of man from
his primordial complete immersion in a less differentiated
social and cultural context. The art, religion, lore, work,
ritual, and myth that were in the archaic past of a single
complex have become gradually "sealed off" from each other,
as Greenberg put it (1953a, p. 562).

But the process of alienation, instead of being regarded
as an increasing estrangement of man from the sources of
his being, or a "sealing off" of activities from one another,
can be viewed as an increasing awareness, or *consciousness*,
on the part of man. Through differentiation, he becomes

conscious of what he was formerly unaware of. And in so doing, he lays the ground for what he will in turn become conscious of at a subsequent stage. Sidney Hook's interpretation is along these lines:

> Hegel understood by self-alienation the process of dialectical development by which the individual consciousness progresses from innocence to maturity, from the simplicity of pure perception to the richly funded comprehension of a complexly interrelated system. Remove the mystification about the Absolute Self, drop the consolatory religious overtones about the meaningfulness of the Whole, and what we get in the language of a barbarous literary psychology is an account of the travail of the human spiritual growth in any culture—not only for the artist but for every human being. (*Partisan Review* Symposium, 1952c, p. 571)

In reacting to present strains, very few intellectuals recommend carrying de-differentiation, or reducing alienation, all the way back (and why stop with Sapir's primitive man? why not go all the way to the primeval ooze?). Most of them recommend stopping at some stage where the advantages of modern society may be purportedly retained and its "undesirable" aspects eliminated. Thus Eliot, while wanting to "retain" ("return to") a stable class structure and the charm of satellite cultures such as Wales, nevertheless recognizes the advantages of differentiation between culture (in its humanistic sense) and religion.

> [When religion is] the *whole way of life* of a people . . . that way of life is also its culture . . . when this identification is complete, it means in actual societies both an inferior culture and an inferior religion. (1948, p. 31)

> The identity of religion and culture remains on the unconscious level, upon which we have superimposed a conscious structure wherein religion and culture are contrasted and can be opposed. . . . To the unconscious level we constantly tend to revert, as we find consciousness an excessive burden; and the tendency towards reversion may explain the powerful attraction which totalitarian philosophy and practice can exert upon humanity. Totalitarianism appeals to the desire to return to the womb. The contrast between religion and culture imposes a strain: we escape from this strain by attempting to revert to an identity of religion and culture which prevailed at a more primitive stage. (p. 68)

What he has had to say on *this* matter is strikingly similar to our own point of view. The identification of religion and culture means that both are inferior because one is ascribed to the other; the development of one is tied to the requirements of the other. Their differentiation has required a distinction at the conscious level that previously was not necessary, but both can fulfill their functions more adequately because they can be contrasted and opposed. The strain of making the conscious distinction is, however, an excessive burden (the strain of upgrading) and we tend to revert (regress) to the stage when it was not necessary. The strain of the contrast between the two (the strain of integration) also induces a regression to a less differentiated stage. The processes that Eliot has detailed here for culture apply as well, in my opinion, to society and to personality.

Another feature of romanticizing the past—in addition to the "loss of wholeness"—is the ignoring of the phenomenon of *extensity*—the spread of gains over larger proportions of the population—that structural differentiation brings about. This type of distortion occurs when the proportion of the population idealized in the past was considerably smaller than the one with which it is compared now. As Greenberg rightly points out, "It is forgotten that only a small proportion of traditional work was done by craftsmen; most of it was labor, drudgery, in town as well as country, and of a kind demanding even less use of the intelligence than does factory work" (1953b, p. 58).

Similar nostalgia is expressed for the close integration of learned men in the seventeenth and eighteenth centuries, when they shared together a common body of knowledge and knew what each other was doing. The overwhelming extension since that time both in the proportion of scholars and of the body of knowledge is either played down or regarded as unfortunate!

With regard to this "cultural longing," Ortega remarks:

In the drawing-room gatherings of last century there inevitably arrived a moment when the ladies and their tame poets put this question, one to the other, "At what period of history would you like to have lived?" And straightaway each of them, making a bundle of his own personal existence, started off on an imaginary tramp along the roads of history in search of a period into which that existence might most delightfully fit. (1950, p. 25)

If one were to add to such a question the qualification that the answerer would have to take the random chance of being *anyone* in the society of the past he chose to live in (and assuming he knew what the society was like), few, I imagine, would have dared venture from their present circumstances. Even Athens had its slaves; the elite were usually less extensively distributed in past ages.

C. P. Snow, in talking about his grandfather who was a maintenance foreman in a tramway depot, said that the "industrial revolution looked very different according to whether one saw it from above or below. . . . To people like my grandfather, there was no question that the industrial revolution was less bad than what had gone before. The only question was, how to make it better" (1959, p. 29).

Industrialisation is the only hope of the poor. I use the word "hope" in a crude and prosaic sense. I have not much use for the moral sensibility of anyone who is too refined to use it so. It is all very well for us, sitting pretty, to think that all material standards of living don't matter much. It is all very well for one, as a personal choice, to reject industrialism—do a modern Walden, if you like, and if you go without much food, see most of your children die in infancy, despise the comforts of literacy, accept twenty years off your own life, then I respect you for the strength of your aesthetic revulsion. But I don't respect you in the slightest if, even passively, you try to impose the same choice on others who are not free to choose. In fact, we know what their choice would be. For with singular unanimity, in any country where they have had the chance, the poor have walked off the land into the factories as fast as the factories could take them. (p. 27)

It was no fun being an agricultural labourer in the mid- to late eighteenth century, in the time that we, snobs that we are, think only of the Enlightenment and Jane Austen. (pp. 28-29)

Snow goes on to speak of another revolution—the scientific revolution that he dates not earlier than thirty to forty years ago:

I believe the industrial society of electronics, atomic energy, automation, is in cardinal respects different in kind from any that has gone before, and will change the world much more. It is this transformation that in my view, is entitled to the name of "scientific revolution." (p. 31)

At least one of its consequences will be, as we have suggested, an even more drastic reduction of routine work by human beings and an increasing demand for their competence at higher levels. Contrary to some popular (and, I think, fantastic) opinion, machines that "think" require humans that think even more. Nor are such machines going to be operated and maintained by a mere handful of top scientists. Our data on the sharp increase of scientists, engineers, technicians, and mathematicians support this view.

The Question of Consumption

We have seen that the moralizers have asserted not only that the individual has lost his old values and his ability to think for himself but that he has—in the process—become self-indulgent. His standard of living has become a "standard of having," as MacLeish expresses it in his television drama (Lottman, 1960). Similarly, the interest that college students express in getting a home in the suburbs with all the appurtenances is considered as an aspiration "for material gratifications for themselves and their families" (quoted in Kluckhohn, 1958, p. 164).

The reformers also take a dim view of the allegedly current emphasis on consumption. If they do not consider the consumer as victimized by the anonymous authority of public opinion, they at least, see him as "lulled by abundance." Whether "lulled by abundance" or "abandoned to hedonism," the relation of the individual to this age of affluence can perhaps be put in a somewhat different perspective.

The issue of personal consumption expenditures centers

predominantly around those made by the family in and for the home. I have not read any statements that would lead me to believe (nor do I think that any social critics would contend) that the issue concerns excessive consumer spending outside of the family context (except that of expense-account spending, and that is not a central issue here).

The principal function of the family is the socialization of children and the personality-management of both its adult and child members. With structural differentiation, the family has been freed from fulfilling other functions (such as economic ones) and has been able to perform its principal function more effectively. If our interpretation of the current strain is correct, the family plays an increasingly important part in the society as the needs of personality development become increasingly paramount. In the context of *consumption*, we may see two ways in which family expenditures on consumers' goods and services can be said to contribute to the development of personality.

First, the concept of "consumption" has to be put in its proper reference. What is consumption from the standpoint of the *economy*—that is, goods and services going *to* households and individuals—is not necessarily consumption, particularly in the hedonistic sense, for those who *buy* them. The purchase of household appliances (kitchen appliances, sewing machines, laundry equipment, and so on), for example, is the purchase of *resources*, or factors of production, for the household; the appliances have been bought with funds that could have been spent on beer and skittles, but instead were plowed back into "plant equipment." As factors of production, they make the household more capital-intensive and routinize the performance of lower-level tasks so that human effort can be liberated for higher-level activities. This type of capitalization represents at least the possibility for an *upgrading of the level of performance* for family members. And the proportion of personal consumption expenditures spent on such goods increased from 1947 to 1956.

Second, we have pointed out that with the upgrading of

demands for performance, the problem of handling emotional needs is also intensified. With the family performing its function of personality-management with more complete differentiation from occupational roles and extended kinship ties, greater permissiveness in the gratification of emotional needs may be allowed in the family without detriment to other functions. Thus, consumer expenditures on such needs in the home are not wholly without justification, unless one holds that greater demands are *not* being made on individuals and that working with other people is in itself a hedonistic process of "smooth adjustment."

With regard to the *proportion* of income spent on *all* consumer needs, the following statements from the Office of Business Economics are of some interest:

[After the immediately postwar buying spree passed] the spending-income ratio averaged 94½ per cent in the 1948-1950 period and 92½ per cent from 1951 to 1957. In none of the 7 years of the latter span did the ratio differ from the average by as much as one percentage point.

The consumer market throughout the postwar period absorbed around two-thirds of total gross national product. This share was lower than that which prevailed in prosperous prewar years when three-fourths of the total output flowed through consumer channels.

[Because of increased government services, of which some did go for increased civilian services, *and* the step-up in government taxation,] the ratio of disposable personal income to GNP was thereby lowered; and, in turn, there was a corresponding reduction in the ratio of consumption to GNP as individuals in the past decade spent and saved roughly the same proportions of their after-tax incomes as they did in the prewar era. (1958, pp. 3-4)

The comments of an economist, Simon Kuznets, on the place of consumption in a national economy give an additional perspective. After pointing out that the share of flow of goods to consumers have been consistently high *throughout* the available history of the American economy, he goes on to say:

But the small share of net capital formation and of the *physically* durable components of the flow of goods to consumers should not be interpreted to mean that current consumption of perishable goods does not contribute to the future capacity of the economy. Indeed, one may argue that its effect is at least as great as that of additions to commodity capital in either business enterprises or households. For a country's greatest capital asset is its people, with their skill, experience, and drive toward useful economic activity. To keep these at a high level the flow of perishable commodities and of services (as well as the flow of goods to consumers in general) is crucial. The effects of a high standard of living, assured by an adequate flow of perishable and other commodities, and of the skills generated by such a "perishable" service as education, are, of course, immense. Hence, even if we forget that, after all, national income is for the consumer and not the consumer for national income; even if we look upon national income chiefly as a means to accumulate capital and augment the country's future productive capacity, substantial portions of the flow of goods to consumers, whether in the perishable or the more durable categories, should be treated as comparable in importance to net capital formation. (1946, p. 20)

In *The Affluent Society*, Galbraith also emphasizes the development of human resources:

However, with the development of a great and complex industrial plant, and even more with the development of a great and sophisticated body of basic science and of experience in its application, . . . modern economic activity requires a greater number of trained and qualified people. Investment in human beings is, *prima facie*, as important as investment in material capital. (1958, pp. 271-72)

Galbraith, however, has taken the position that, because essential needs were long since taken care of, consumers' wants are now created by advertising and emulation. In what he calls the "dependence effect," the higher level of production has to have a higher level of want creation necessitating a higher level of want satisfaction. His point of view, here, is similar to that of the reformers in the implication that there is no consumer sovereignty and also in the suggestion that he, or someone else, can say what man's "essential" needs are. If what he means is that man can do without some things more easily than others, I would agree; but even in that case, the decision as to what commodities should be eliminated is a highly debatable one.

One of Galbraith's main points is that we are not diverting enough of our gross national product for public resources and publicly rendered services. His argument is a cogent one, but the question is—or so it seems to me—one of allocating limited resources and *not* one of condemning consumption expenditures as such. In order to justify buying a new suit instead of a chair, it does not seem necessary to establish the fact that chairs are not really needed after all. In addition, I think that Galbraith, like the reformers, overrates the power of advertising, but that is another topic.

Mass Culture

The impact of advertising on individual choice is but one aspect of the larger issue of mass culture, which is seen as cheapening the standards of choice. It is claimed that mass culture presents representations of human beings— whether in advertisements or on the telescreen, in the press or on film—that provide slick models of personality that the public emulates, unwittingly or not. Since mass culture caters to the widest market, so the argument goes, it pitches its content to the lowest common denominator of understanding so that few discriminations and subtleties are drawn for fear of losing part of the audience. What should be a vehicle for enriching human experience becomes, instead, a banal reiteration of the meretricious.

Any capacity that the public might have, it is said, for appreciating the variety and quality of life and of art is not only left undeveloped but is deadened; for accessibility to anything that requires active effort is shunned in favor of the narcotizing ease with which mass culture may be passively absorbed. As in Macdonald's reference to Gresham's law (which I have extended to characterize other allegations as well), the cheap and easy drive out the worthwhile and the difficult.

According to this theory, then, not only is the content of mass culture itself characterized by a lack of discrimination and diversity, but its audience is so characterized as well. On the one hand, the content is, as Macdonald puts it, "homogenized": everything is mixed and scrambled together. On the other hand, the audience is an aggregate of mass men, *"solitary* atom[s], *uniform and undifferentiated* from thousands and millions of other atoms who go to make up 'the lonely crowd'" [my italics] (1957, p. 69).

We have, then, not just an implicit assumption but an overt assertion that mass culture is transmitted "massively" by mass media to a mass audience. There is the "predominant view that there is almost a one-to-one relationship between the content of the media and their impact on the public" (Bauer and Bauer, 1961, p. 12), or between mass culture and the masses, as it was expressed in our formulation in Chapter 5. Given such an assumption, any statement about one side of the relationship enables one to make a statement about the other side without having to consider it independently; that is, if A and B are a one-to-one relationship, one can talk about B solely on the basis of knowledge of A, or vice versa.

In the ideological versions we discussed, we saw that each considers the relationship to work one way: both elitists and moralizers believe that the demand of the masses determines the standards of mass culture. The reformers believe that the content of mass culture determines the standards of the masses. Finally, we saw that Macdonald has suggested that neither is "causal" but that the relationship is like a reciprocating engine.

In attacking this problem, the first step is not to assume any such simple one-to-oneness but to examine the extent to which each component may be independent of the other. As Daniel Bell pointed out, the theory of mass culture starts out, instead, by eliminating the distinction between two things:

. . . a judgment as to the *quality* of modern experience [mass culture]—with much of which any sensitive individual would agree—and a presumed scientific statement concerning the disorganization of society created by industrialization [the reformers' focus on alienation] and by the demands of the masses for equality [the elitists' focus]. (1956, p. 77)

With this in mind, we will first investigate the problem of the masses from the two points of view: 1) the extent to which they are "disorganized solitary atoms"—a social-structure problem—so that their standards are determined by mass culture and 2) the extent to which their low standards—a "value" problem—determine mass culture itself. We will then focus neither on the masses nor on their standards but on cultural content in general.

The Social Structure of the Audience.—With regard to the reformers' allegation that the recipients of mass culture are an aggregate of isolated, undifferentiated, and solitary atoms, there are two assumptions: 1) that the individual receives "messages" via the mass media as an isolated person without reference to other persons with whom he has meaningful relations; and 2) that the content of the message—be it an effort to influence a vote or a purchase, a model of what is considered appropriate behavior, or a conception of what is considered artistic or entertaining—has a direct impact on the individual. It determines his standards of choice with regard to that content and without reference to any other standards.

A steadily accumulating body of sociological investigation has seriously challenged both of these assumptions. At least two surveys of the extensive (but still inadequate) research done in this area have been made: one by Bauer and Bauer (1961) and the other by Riley and Riley (1959). Both surveys summarize the studies that have investigated radio listening and television watching habits, newspaper and magazine reading habits. They list research that has looked into the impact of mass communication on decisions to vote and to buy consumer goods, into the effect of concerted efforts to change public opinion, or propaganda in general.

The evidence these studies have adduced indicates that the recipient of mass communication cannot be characterized as an isolated and massified person. On the contrary, his

perception of and response to the mass-communicated message is made with reference to others with whom he has
face-to-face, or primary, relationships.

> It becomes apparent that the consumer faced with a baffling array
> of brands, the voter choosing between political courses with un-
> known consequences, and the entertainment-seeker with untold pos-
> sibilities on his television dial make choices which are not based
> primarily on the inherent merits of the object chosen—no matter
> how persuasively these merits may have been advertised to them.
> It further appears that these choices are widely affected, not alone
> by the choice object itself or by advertising and propaganda about
> it, but also by other people. The individual often decides to pur-
> chase or to vote or to look at television programs *with* trusted other
> people, rather than *for* a particular brand or candidate or program.
> Thus his reactions are not random relative to the reactions of these
> others. His perceptions and reactions form part of a pattern of inter-
> actions and mutual orientations among all members of the group.
> (Riley and Riley, 1959, p. 552)

One might say, on reading the above statement, that the
evidence merely confirms the widespread conformity that
the intellectuals have alleged to exist. If such is the case,
then the individual cannot be *both* a conformist *and* an
atomized mass-man at the same time. Further evidence,
however, indicates that "the individual belongs and refers,
not to just one group, but to many" (Riley and Riley, 1959).
As in the case of the criss-crossing solidarities that obtain
among intermediate relationships, there are "countervailing
powers," so to speak, so that one's standards are not shaped
by one reference group alone.

Bauer and Bauer, moreover, cite studies to the effect that
reference groups are not the flat, undifferentiated aggregates
of approval-seekers that the intellectuals sometimes suggest
they are. Within such groups are opinion leaders who mediate "between the media and the broad mass of the population" (1961, p. 26). Moreover, opinion leaders are not a
single type of person. "They varied with the subject matter
under consideration. They exercised their influence in varying fashion. The flow of influence was not always 'down-
wards,' but sometimes 'upwards' and 'sidewards.' The network

of communications is a *socially structured one depending upon established patterns of social relations* [my italics]" (1961, p. 27).

The Quality of Demand.—The value-oriented wing of ideological thought holds that mass culture is due to the low standards of the masses. We discussed this point of view primarily with reference to the elitist version, which assumes that the masses are not qualified to set standards and should not presume to wrest that responsibility from a qualified elite. This is another way of saying that the ability of any member of the non-elite to become a member of the elite cannot be taken for granted; membership in the elite is a special status for which each individual must prove himself worthy, like entering orders in the Roman Catholic Church.

The moralizers, of course, agree with elitists that the low quality of mass culture is due to the low quality of demand, but they think it is possible to upgrade the non-elite to elite standards. Elitists look with scorn on such "uplifting" notions and call them middlebrowism. *Life* magazine runs series on art, Leonard Bernstein explains music over television, and now even the *Saturday Evening Post* and *Esquire* mediate highbrow condemnations of middlebrowism to a middlebrow audience. The moralizers think this is all to the good. But it is anathema to the elitists, who regard these efforts as just one more watering-down of high culture.

Within the allegations about the low quality of mass demand, there are at least three issues that must be sorted out if anything approaching a clear understanding of the situation is to be attempted. The intellectuals have a tendency to homogenize them.

1) comparisons with the past
2) the problem of extensity
3) the alleged dilution of high culture

First, in order to assess the actual quality of contemporary mass culture, some reference point must be chosen. It may be compared with an ideal state of affairs, in which case *any* judgment at *any* time is bound to discover inadequacy. But in order to put the present into perspective, some reference to the past must be made. Is the present "better" or "worse" than the past? If it is better, does the rate of improvement come up to expectations?

Among many others, Shils (1957) has pointed out that contemporary mass culture is not only no worse but is possibly even better than the "mass culture" of past times (or what critics charmingly call "folk culture," although they make, of course, a distinction between its rural and urban manifestations). He reminds us not only of bear-baiting and cock-fighting and of the widespread superstition that prevailed during ages of reason and enlightenment but also of the quality of "mass" literature that flourished from the Middle Ages to the nineteenth century.

Fabliaux and *colportage,* broadside ballads and chapbooks were scarcely more wholesome than today's most lurid paperbacks and horror comics. They were characterized as well by salaciousness, vulgarity, and often sadistic violence. What is perhaps worse, they purveyed their content under the guise of being morally uplifting, thus lending the salacious a spurious legitimation.

In addition, high culture itself was not all Shakespeare, Jonson, Bacon, Hobbes, Racine, *et al.* Shils goes on to say:

No one who has spent many hours in old libraries or in antiquarian bookshops can evade the conclusion that the vast majority of books produced in the 17th and 18th centuries, to say nothing of the 19th century, were of no consequence from an aesthetic, moral, or intellectual point of view. . . . [There were] a far greater number of absolutely worthless writers, authors of spurious philosophical works, of foolishly mean-spirited and trivial theological treatises, of tales as vapid as the choices of the Book of the Month Club and of poems which would try even the insensate patience of a Ph.D. candidate in English literature. (1957, pp. 605-6)

Second, as we saw in our discussion of romanticizing the past, any assessment of the present must account for the proportion of the population referred to now in terms of that referred to in the past. In previous centuries, nothing other than the "folk" culture of which we spoke was accessible to the masses.

The culture of these strata, which were dulled by labor, illness, and fear . . . comprised a far larger proportion of the population than they do in advanced societies of the 20th century. . . . (Shils, 1957, p. 604)

Thanks to the industrial revolution, these lower strata have now come on to the market, so to speak; the inaccessibility of non-folk forms of cultural participation has steadily declined.

Perhaps the growth of mass culture in Europe is a result of the fact that, for the first time, the lower classes have enough money and time to make their demands in the culture market felt. Perhaps "Americanization" is merely a rise in the standard of living of the masses and a narrowing of the gap between the classes. (Lipset, 1960, p. 329)

This state of affairs is, of course, precisely what the elitist critics deplore as an invasion by the untutored. The standards of those newly arrived on the non-folk cultural scene are, to varying degrees, below elite standards. But they are being *judged in terms of those standards.* Apart from the impact on high culture that this "invasion" may or may not have had, it must be remembered that the judgment is being applied to an overwhelming majority of the population (at least in America), who are expected to measure up to the standards of an elite, a handful of the population in past times.

Third, does the expansion of the cultural market dilute high culture? If one grants that mass culture "mines" high culture for ideas, that mass culture simplifies, abridges, or lengthens the content of high culture so that it may presumably be made accessible to a large audience, does this distortion change the nature of what is distorted? Does the representation of Shakespeare's work on television change the nature of that work any more than did Charles and Mary Lamb's *Tales*? Ideas and art forms, like symphonic melodies transformed into popular tunes, may temporarily and in certain quarters become vulgarized and threadbare, but they are surely not "consumed" in the process. Nor is the highbrow compelled to watch or listen if he finds it distasteful.

The intellectuals contend that the audience, subjected to popularized versions of high culture with its built-in reactions, is prevented from approaching the work in its pristine form. Instead, the audience learns to perceive it in oversimplified terms, not realizing that a fuller appreciation may be had or not wanting to make the effort that it requires. If such is the case, one can at least ask if popularized high culture is not preferable to horror comics.

Perhaps it is not unfair to point out that the intellectuals themselves are rather adept at building in reactions and oversimplifying distinctions when they write social criticism. They are not completely innocent of dramatizing the black and white aspects of their material with exaggerated effects designed to titillate the hostilities of their audience. The culturemongers are not the only ones who know how to play to the gallery. Some of our more clever writers have perhaps qualified for their position as social critics on the basis of such a talent. But then, of course, literary style is more "cultural" than reliable analysis.

To return to the intellectuals' allegations about the downgrading of culture through popularization, the "masses" cannot be expected to attain an understanding of high culture by one grand leap from non-elitism to elitism. Standards of appreciation, criteria of discrimination must be acquired and developed in stages. The educational material presented by the mass media is perhaps no worse and much of it is better than that introduced in many secondary schools—in Europe as well as in America—where many learn to loathe what others come to cherish. Moreover, as has been frequently pointed out, many persons who are introduced to high culture at popularized levels are stimulated to press further and learn more than has been offered to them. They not only wish to fill in the gaps that simplified versions leave vacant, but they are made aware of those gaps by other people. As in the case of multiple membership in primary groups, their contact with "culture" is often not limited to one flat level of banality. The intellectuals themselves perform an important function in this respect by pointing out the inadequacies of too facile and slick an approach.

Insofar as upgrading the cultural standards is concerned, a crucially important force is what is now popularly referred to as status-seeking, or what Riesman more subtly refers to as acquiring the "right" consumption preferences. Many people make the effort to acquire a familiarity with better music and art, with the theater and with literature, in order to share tastes and experiences with groups they belong to or aspire to. In so doing, whatever their motives may be, they are introduced to an area of cultural participation that they often subsequently enjoy. One may dismiss this, if he chooses, as a crass desire to acquire the requisite insignia of status. But one can also interpret it as another example of the way in which social structure maintains and raises standards, exerts a leverage on the individual to live up to those standards, and thus prevents Gresham's law from operating.

Many have pointed out, Russell Lynes (1949) as well as others, that the criteria of status have shifted to some extent from economic reference—where "taste" was primarily a means for ostentatiously asserting affluence—to an esthetic and cultural reference—where questions of style and of form and canons of criticism prevail in their own right.

Although it may be a matter of opinion, I agree with Kluckhohn when he says that "there is abundant evidence that popular taste in the United States is improving" (1958, p. 193). The present era stands up very well indeed when contrasted with the pompous overstatement of the Victorian period or the self-conscious revolt of the twenties with its *beaux-arts* modernity. Nor should the measure of extensity be overlooked. While the present era may not produce the fine craftsmanship of earlier periods (and the contention that craftsmanship has vanished is not a foregone conclusion), today's mass-produced furnishings for the home, for example, are an incontestable improvement over the goods of meretricious design (referred to as "borax" in the trade) that glutted the market only a few decades ago.

To summarize, one need only quote Kluckhohn's data to show that an upgrading process in the quality of cultural standards has been going on:

. . . there has been a remarkable diversification and broadening of the base of leisure-time activities within the population. Between 1940 and 1950 ticket sales for the legitimate theatre and the opera went up 85 per cent as against only 42 per cent for motion pictures. Attendance at concerts of serious music jumped 88 per cent; more dollars were spent for them in 1951 than for baseball. By 1951 there were 659 symphonic groups in the United States, and the number of towns and cities having regular concert series had doubled since 1940. Sales of paintings, attendance at art museums, the number of art museums had increased at an almost fantastic rate. The sales of art supplies were ten times as great in 1949 as in 1939. Gardening, photography, *participation* in sports, foreign travel—all gained fabulously. (1958, pp. 192-3)

Technology.—In Chapter 5, we reviewed the intellectuals' misgivings about technology. Technology, it will be recalled, has an impact on the quality of both demand and supply. On the one hand they say, it makes cultural content accessible to an increasingly broader audience; thus, they view not only television and public education with some qualms, but one commentator referred to even writing itself as a means whereby culture became available to those of doubtful qualification (Emerson secundus, 1950, p. 137). The preceding section has attempted to deal with the problems that this allegation raises by pointing out the process of upgrading that accompanies such a broadening of the cultural base.

On the other hand, technology is said to cheapen the quality of cultural content because it encourages producers to be preoccupied with technological pyrotechnics of various kinds. That this consequence is empirically possible is undeniable; that it frequently occurs is undoubtedly the case.

It should, however, be noted that the quality of content and
technological possibilities are not connected in a zero-sum
relationship. High technological capacity does not necessarily
mean low quality. As Rabbaseire points out, "The technical
characteristics of printing, filming, broadcasting, televising,
recording do not restrict, but enlarge the range of our experience and the possibilities of expression" (1956a, p. 332).
We should be grateful to all critics who restrain those producers who would be lured into substituting technique for
quality, but we may doubt their conclusion that technology
itself is the sole villain.

A *Note on Cultural Diversity.*—Another aspect or result
of "mass culture" currently lamented is the loss of regional
and ethnic diversity. Sapir's comment on United States as
a "flat cultural morass" comes to mind, as does Eliot's wish
to retain the charm of satellite cultures such as Wales. In
one respect, their assessment of modern society is correct:
regional diversities do tend to diminish; and the more complex societies become, the more they *tend* to become like
one another as *total* societies. This proposition is in line with
Durkheim's notion that there are more differences between
primitive societies—from one *society* to another—and fewer
between more complex societies. Durkheim draws an illuminating analogy with the biological world, where there is an
infinite variety of the lower forms of life but there is only one
homo sapiens (1949, p. 137).

But we must also remember Durkheim's observation that
in any given primitive society (no matter how charmingly
unique it may be), there are more resemblances among the
individuals who compose it (p. 133). And their cultural
characteristics are highly ascribed to the social structure.
Thus, the cultural uniqueness that intellectuals discover in
regions or among ethnic groups is one that is ascribed to that
region or group, one that admits of little opportunity for its
individual members to be different. Frequently the assimila-
tion of such "sub-cultures" into the larger whole results not
in a disappearance of their particular folkways but in an

incorporation and a diffusion of them through the larger society. The changes that have come about since the end of World War II in American eating habits and in the variety of goods—many of diverse ethnic origins—offered in almost any supermarket reflect such a process.

Conclusion: Mass Culture.—There is, then, perhaps a further process of differentiation going on in the society with respect to the esthetic aspects of behavior—those aspects concerned with style and form, with what is appropriately expressive, with what is broadly referred to as taste. We are concerned here with the extent to which their expression is increasingly becoming emancipated from ascription to structural features of the society.

The preceding discussion has touched on several areas where such emancipation may be said to be going on. With the decrease of regional and ethnic differences, culture is less ascribed to particular areas and groups; with the emancipation of the personality not only from class but from family as well, the individual's choice of taste and of style is less predetermined. He does not, as Greenberg claimed, necessarily acquire an ingrained sense of proportion from the family during childhood, at least insofar as access to culture and taste are concerned. There are too many people who have transcended limited family backgrounds for that idea to carry much weight anymore.

It is, of course, this very freedom from ascription in this area of choice that has led to the preoccupation with what Riesman has called consumption preferences. What some have called conformity to the tastes of others, I have called an effort to develop sensitivity by gaining access to new standards, and especially by helping to define them. That such exploration may result in uncertainty and anxiety is in the nature of the case and is one of the costs one pays for trying to widen his horizons.

In addition, esthetic standards have perhaps been emancipated to some degree from ascription to economic status, as pointed out in our discussion of status-seeking. That is, they are less an ostentatious means of proving that one has "arrived" than enjoyments for their own sakes. One can say with more certainty that they have been emancipated from the restrictions of a more provincial and philistine past where interest in the cultural was left to women and considered foppish for men and sissy for boys. Despite the revolt of the twenties against philistinism—an ideological movement spearheaded by intellectuals and for which they may deservedly take much of the credit—it is possibly only since the last war that this opprobrium has been substantially shaken off.

These considerations bring us to the problem of why many more intellectuals have embraced the more conservative elitist version of mass culture when—in other respects—their posture is considerably more liberal. Even the reformers' ideology is elitist in that in its lament over the "loss of community," it implies that "folk culture" should be maintained. Thus, we see the paradox of some former radical intellectuals now asserting that a stable class structure is a desirable social arrangement!

The explanation of the shift to an elitist point of view may lie in the fact that the current ideological issue has moved into the very field where the intellectual considers himself the elite. He sets the cultural standards. When the issues were concerned with economic and political questions, he was combatting forces over which people in his then social position had little control. He was in favor of emancipating the individual from ascription to economic and political elites; thus he took a liberal posture. But now certain cultural standards themselves are being emancipated from ascription to cultural elites; his own hegemony is being threatened. I am not suggesting that this necessarily represents the intellectuals' desire to retain "power," for it can also represent the uneasiness of an overprotective parent who is loath to let the children become independent—and, in the consequence, make mistakes along the way.

The loss of control in this area, coupled with the competition the intellectual is now getting from sociologists (see

Chapter 10) as interpreters of contemporary experience, may cause him to "develop a nostalgia for a past era when [he] did not face this competition, and for other less differentiated societies, such as exist in both England and France" (Parsons, 1959a, p. 494). Such a reference is likely to take the form of yearning for a more aristocratic, class-defined world.

That the members of society are capable of internalizing appropriate standards, of upgrading them, and of acting autonomously has been the purport of the argument throughout this section. The elite will have to become—willingly or unwillingly—a "lost-object," to use Freud's term, in the same way that parents do.

In a more theoretical vein, something more might be said about the elitist type of conservatism among some of the reformers, who have always prided themselves on their radically liberal stance. Their conception of their role with respect to cultural standards has an ideological resemblance to the Marxian role of the intellectuals or the Party as an elite with respect to political standards and organization. (I am, of course, comparing similarities of ideological thought-patterns and *not* suggesting that the same people subscribe to the same beliefs in both cases.)

According to Marxian thought, the inexorable dialectic will eventually bring about the classless society. Under this desirable social condition, no elite agency will be required to set and maintain standards. Given the proper conditions, standards are no longer problematical. However, an elite—whether it be intellectuals bringing class-consciousness to the proletariat or the Party organizing the society—can presumably quicken the process and help the dialectic along until the proper social conditions are attained. When they are arrived at, the Party will no longer be necessary: the state will wither away.

With respect to the mass-culture problem, the reformers seem to share a similar belief that cultural standards could be taken for granted if only the proper social conditions prevailed. Under such conditions, the mass of men will assert their cultural autonomy and the guidance of an elite, like the state, will wither away. But until that time, reformers may embrace elitism as an intermediate means to hold the line. Indeed, the alleged undesirability of current conditions makes it more urgent. The failure of the masses—no matter how improved their lot may be—to assert their cultural autonomy is seen as a direct consequence of their being victimized by a hostile power structure. No matter how much more money or time the masses may have, ideal factors such as cultural standards cannot escape the determinism of the "real" power factors. Or so it is claimed.

Conformity

All discussions about conformity seem to start at the same point. One must ask: conforming to what? how can we compare currently reported conformity with the past? Lipset has made an effort to answer the latter question by studying reports on American society by Tocqueville, Harriet Martineau, the Trollopes, Bryce, and others. He came to the conclusion that conformity, Whyte's social ethic, and Riesman's other-directedness have not basically reversed the pattern of American life which the nineteenth-century foreign travelers saw as uniquely American (1960, pp. 409-12).

There are perhaps two aspects to what intellectual spokesmen—and the public that has picked up the term—mean by conformity. (I refer here to its symptoms, not to the imputations the intellectuals make about its underlying reasons.) One aspect is uniformity of behavior; the other is the desire to seek others' approval, to be a "smooth adjuster." These aspects may exist independently of each other or together.

With regard to uniformity, I would suggest that much of it represents a routinization of lower-level choices. In view of the increased intensity of social interaction and of the demands made on those interacting to "come to terms" in new and different ways, the standardization of certain patterns of behavior not essentially significant in human intercourse liberates the attention for more important considerations. It liberates the attention of the individual in his not having to make certain decisions about his own actions and also in not being distracted by departures from routine procedures in others. Perhaps Whyte had something like this in mind when he pointed out that "surface uniformities can serve quite well as protective coloration . . . a sensible awareness of the rules of the game can be a condition of individualism as well as a constraint upon it" (1956, p. 12).

It is, of course, difficult to draw a line here, but certain general standards of appearance, of manner, of actions that are included in what are known as the social amenities, fall within this routine category. It is often at this level that self-conscious efforts to assert "individuality" take the form of Bohemianism or eccentricity. Whatever function they may perform for the individual concerned, they usually do not require a great amount of originality.

The evidence in this area is largely intuitive and based on commentators' personal experience, and it is difficult to say whether there has been an increase in uniformity, in this respect, or not. In terms of extensity, there has no doubt been an increase in another kind of uniformity. With a larger proportion of persons living in urban centers and earning incomes in the middle ranges, with the wider distribution of mass-produced goods and services, more people have been placed in similar circumstances so that their behavior at certain levels becomes more alike. But are these similarities in themselves significant indicators of *individuality?* They may instead be significant for individuality in that they represent the reduction of *ascribed* differences—such as differences in class, income, and region—and an expansion of opportunities to be different at more meaningful levels.

The second aspect of conformity—the preoccupation with what other people think and approve of—may represent an effort to understand the nature of one's relationships with other people and, in so doing, to discover the "self" in the looking-glass of others' reactions; to use Cooley's metaphor, "Each to each a looking-glass/reflects the other that doth _pass" (1902, p. 184). If indeed the personality is characterized by the kinds of relationships one has had in the past, a crucial aspect of it lies in the manner in which one relates to others. By means of these relationships, he is able to enrich his own personal experience through being able to grasp that of others. Heightened awareness of personal experience, one of the joys to be had by reading literature, is surely accessible as well through interaction with others, even though in some respects it is more difficult. Self-awareness, by definition, means, among other things, becoming aware of what one is doing, as the psychoanalyst Sullivan and others have pointed out. It is perhaps one of the ironies of life that others often know more about the patterns of behavior an individual habitually follows than he does himself.

Personality disturbance, when present to a sufficient degree, often distinguishes an individual as being a "character," "different," or—from some points of view—"interesting." However engaging others may find such idiosyncrasy, it is scarcely the result of individual autonomy. On the contrary, an ascription to past circumstances in fact restricts the individual from becoming what he might be, from perceiving new ranges of choice and learning new ways of making choice.

In this connection, it is frequently said, for example, that psychoanalysis is undesirable because it deprives a person of his individuality. I suspect that many analysts would be highly gratified if they were consistently able to deprive their patients of the types of "individuality" that bring them to their couches. Norman Mailer expresses one of the more extreme views along this line:

In practice, psychoanalysis has by now become all too often no more than a psychic blood-letting. The patient is not so much changed as aged, and the infantile fantasies which he is encouraged to express are condemned to exhaust themselves against the analyst's non-responsive reactions. The result for all too many patients is a diminution, a "tranquilizing" of their most interesting qualities and vices. . . . He is able to conform to that contradictory and unbearable society which first created his neurosis. (1957, p. 283)

Our argument is, however, no special plea for psychoanalysis but rather an attempt to point out that much of what passes for anxiety about other persons' opinions and approval may very well be an effort to understand and develop one's personality, an effort of increased importance in view of the demands being made on it to work with others in a complex society. What Fromm has called the "indiscriminate talking about one's problems" (1955b, p. 157), Daniel Lerner has referred to as follows:

A mobile society required a mobile personality, a self-system so adaptive to change that rearrangement is its permanent mode. It required the experience of psychic mobility through many generations to evolve participant institutions which, to ordinary men, felt "normal." The mobile person shows a high capacity for identifying himself with new and strange aspects of the environment. He is capable of handling unfamiliar demands upon himself outside his habitual experience. [He develops] a strong capacity for empathy ("see one's self in the other fellow's situation"). (1958, p. 157)

It should be remembered that this effort to understand personality and interpersonal relationships—what Lerner calls the "capacity for empathy"—may result in empirical failures; the effort may backfire with the consequence of "smooth adjustment" or a crippling preoccupation with others' opinions. But the *interpretation* of these empirical consequences is quite different when one approaches their appraisal from the perspective we have taken here; for one can then see the effort as one that must be made, as one that cannot be abandoned because of its difficulty or dismissed as unnecessary and undesirable. In addition, an element of distortion very likely enters the reporting of the evidence when seen from the ideological point of view, with its tendency to see nothing *but* failure, nothing *but* smooth adjustment, where indeed those persons reported on are accomplishing a great deal more than merely getting along with other people.

Personality and the Family.—In addition to this intensified concern with interpersonal relations, the greater demands on personality are reflected in changing patterns of family life. Intellectuals point out—and often lament—that children are increasingly socialized by agencies outside the home as they become involved in a wide range of organized activities. What seems to many as the incredible latitude given to American children and their overinvolvement in activities away from the home may also be interpreted as encouraging children to become less dependent on their families and learning how to confront new situations with a variety of other people. This aspect of child-rearing is referred to as *independence-training.* Greater permissiveness toward children when they are at home can then be regarded as supplying the emotional support required by the greater demands for performance in contexts where the child is more "on his own."

Of course, the family itself provides the very foundation for the capacity to meet the demands on the personality to understand the complexity of human relations and of personality problems. The concern that college students reveal in their plans for the future—about the homes and the children they plan to have—is not simply a matter of preoccupation with future comfort. A study done by Miriam Johnson (1955), for example, on a sample of college women revealed that those girls who wanted to have the *greatest* number of children were also those who were already looking ahead to the time when their as yet unborn children would enter society as adults. They were thinking in terms of their future children's college education and career plans and how these children could make a contribution to society when they reached maturity.

But the girls who wanted *fewer* children expected to enjoy them in and for themselves. They focussed primarily on the satisfactions of having children and on the enjoyment of family life. It was quite clear that the girls who wanted to rear *larger* families defined their role in life as developing the personalities of their future children so that they in turn could make a worthwhile contribution.

Although based on a small, local sample, Johnson's research on these attitudes is highly suggestive in its implications for our interpretation of what has been going on in American society. It suggests that decisions to have more babies are not to be taken simply as a retreat from achievement in the larger society to the privatistic enjoyment of family life. Having children is not simply another form of consumer activity. On the contrary, it may not be too far-fetched to suggest that rearing larger families, given the attitudes that may underlie such decisions, is one aspect of the rapidly emerging emphasis on *developing human resources*. Moreover, this emphasis represents a further stage of development in American society—a stage different from those that have preceded it, a stage with new problems and challenges. Inherent in it lies the source of our strain: the demands for personality development. The way in which the admittedly slim evidence cited above fits into this picture will be clearer as we go along.

Stages of Development:
From Economy to Personality

We have talked about social change as a structural differentiation that results in greater flexibility in making choices and in greater fluidity of resources. Once emancipated from various forms of ascription, these resources can be combined in a greater variety of ways; desirable goals may be defined and pursued more effectively. This process, however, is not a simple unilinear advance that means more and more of the same thing. One may think of it, rather, as a process going through qualitatively different stages.

These stages do not follow one another in any order whatsoever. Certain types of development must be accomplished and consolidated before others can occur. Just as a human must learn to speak a language in order to go to school, in order to earn a living, and so on; societies, if they are to move from primitive simplicity to modern complexity, must pass through qualitatively different stages. In each stage, different types of resources are recruited, developed, and organized.

In any particular society, obviously, the process will be carried out differently from that in others; "development" may be pushed further in some sectors than in others with the consequence of different kinds of combinations, or "mixes." But in all cases, one can say that certain ingredients are necessary along the way regardless of how they are combined. And one can also say that the "combining" is necessary: the process of development requires progressively complex organization and institutionalization of procedures in the society. The process is, of course, by no means inevitable; the pages of history are replete with cases where it has been arrested or reversed, as well as with cases where it was never set in motion at all.

In *The Stages of Economic Growth* (1960), W. W. Rostow has set forth his conception of this process for economic development as a series of stages he calls the traditional society, preconditions for takeoff, takeoff, drive to maturity, and the age of high mass-consumption. In our terms, what Rostow calls the takeoff is the emancipation of economic resources from traditional ascription and their successful mobilization. Moreover, Rostow does not fall into the trap of treating economic development as if it were, or could be, isolated from the rest of the society. He repeatedly points out that "non-economic" types of resource-development are necessary ingredients if economic development is to take place at all. Economic development requires, for example, technology, the acquisition of technological skills by men, the requisite human motivation, a legal framework to regulate some sort of market system, and—above all—the organization of all these factors and their institutional legitimation. These ingredients are *resources,* too. Although the term resource is more common to economic discourse, I am using the term in its most general sense.

It is beyond the scope of this book to set forth this process of stages of development more thoroughly, but I have presented the above sketch in order to discuss an important aspect of the ideological issue we are confronting. In interpreting what is going on in American society, many commentators have a tendency to base their interpretations on a stage of our development—broadly, the stage of growth to economic maturity—that, in important respects, has now been completed. They see the problems of that stage as relatively solved, its challenges eliminated or at least routinized. I agree. But they fail to see that the problems and challenges now emerging must be thought of in terms of a new and quite different stage. I am not suggesting that these commentators are so naïve that they consider all human and social problems solved, but that the way in which they conceptualize them may lead to misinterpretation. Thus, they tend to assume that social development with its challenges has reached an end-of-the-line and to think of new problems in terms of previous stages, as an extrapolation of economic, or purely political, processes. There are many versions.

Both Riesman (1950) and Rostow (1960), for example, have tended to embrace the end-of-the-line argument. They are quite aware that American society has left one stage behind and is now entering another. For Riesman, the shift is from inner-direction to other-direction; for Rostow, from the drive-to-maturity to the age of high mass-consumption. For both, it is the shift from problems of production to problems of consumption. With the attainment of a mature economy, the problems of production have become relatively solved, the processes of financing and technological advance, routinized. What previously had been a challenge evoking daring innovation by individuals has now become built into society so that it runs more or less automatically. Consumer goods, once scarce, are now embarrassingly plentiful.

To summarize Riesman's formulation: "Where the individual formerly innovated on the frontier of production, he now adjusts to others on the *last* frontier—that of consumption" (Parsons and White, 1961). Rostow's formulation similarly implies an evaporation of challenge. Setting aside the problem of the cold war, he asks, *what lies beyond?* What will happen, he asks, as the shift moves the process another notch forward, and diminishing relative marginal utility sets in, on a mass basis, for real income itself? Will man fall into secular spiritual stagnation, finding no worthy outlet for the expression of his energies, talents, and instinct to reach for immortality? (1960, p. 91)

Americans, Rostow suggests, have to some extent reimposed the strenuous life by raising the birth-rate. They have made "a most extraordinary and unexpected decision . . . [and begun] to behave as if they preferred the extra baby to the extra unit of consumption" (p. 80). That is to say, as diminishing returns on consumers' goods set in, Americans turned to having more babies as an alternate choice. Although Rostow concedes that by rapidly increasing the population, Americans have to some extent reintroduced the problem of scarcity, or "reimposed the strenuous life," he does not seem to regard larger families as a positive contribution to resources, human resources, in the sense I have indicated. He speaks, for example, of larger families as "blandishments" along with durable consumers' goods and services (p. 92).

Significantly, both Riesman and Rostow, as well as others, analyze the new stage from the economic perspective of the previous one. This stage involves the consumption of the resources generated by the previous stage. From the point of view of economic development, consumption is, of course, virtually the end-of-the-line.

The difficulty here is clearly not one of recognizing the "facts" in the case. It is one of interpreting them from a different perspective. The shift is not, I suggest, one from producing economic resources to consuming them. *It is a shift from emphasis on the development of economic resources to the development of human resources*—particularly, the capacities of personalities.

As the earlier section on "consumption" contended, much of what has been interpreted as consumption from the economic perspective can now be seen as an input to the family of facilities for generating new skills, as Kuznets put it. Other-direction may be seen not as trading consumption preferences but as acquiring greater sensitivity to personality problems. This is not meant to imply that human resources have not been essential since the beginning of mankind. It does mean that new, higher-level uses of these resources are now, for the first time, both possible and necessary. The resources of personality, as we have seen, have been emancipated from ascriptive ties in significantly new ways. Durable consumers' goods in the home and automation in the factory and office liberate human effort from tasks of a more physical nature. Upgrading the levels of performance requires greater skills on the job and in more complex interpersonal relationships.

The current preoccupation on the American scene with education is, of course, the most salient symptom of this shift. Education, moreover, is not solely a matter of job-training or "catching up with the Russians." It is also a matter of enlarging the individual's understanding, a capacity of the personality, of the complex world he lives in. This is not news, but it gets lost in the shuffle.

Conclusion

This chapter has attempted to analyze patterns of life that are newly emerging on the American scene, patterns that entail new levels of awareness, of understanding, and of accomplishment. It has tried to show the way in which these changes and the difficulties they raise represent yet another stage in the development of man from prehistoric times. With the accumulation of past experience, these stages have a way of recurring at a faster rate so that now the impact of one is scarcely absorbed before another is upon us.

The impact of the current change on the individual has spread through the society virtually within a lifetime. Unlike previous changes, it must be confronted by the individual independently. It cannot be absorbed *for* the individual by the family, the church, a class, or an economic or political interest. It is one that the individual must confront by making choices without dependence on ascriptive guidance. He is, indeed, forced to be free.

The big question is "free for what?" If it is true that man now has *freedom from* older forms of ties and *freedom to* make a greater variety of choices, what is he going to do with them? Because of the very fact that we are entering this stage of development, we do not know the answer. If we did, we would already be well through it. Just as the economic stage required innovation in the face of uncertainty, so the present one requires another, perhaps more daring, certainly more personal, type of innovation. More important than knowing the answer now is being able to ask the question at all. In his new freedom from ascription, in making choices that define his very identity, the individual is asking "Who am I?" Who can say if he finds it more difficult than primitive man found his struggle for survival, or Reformation man his concern for his immortal soul? It is in the very nature of the choice, to be sure, that modern man does face it independently.

But he does *not* arrive at such independence without the resources that society and its culture make possible. He does not face an absurd, unordered world alone. As paradoxical as it may seem, his opportunities to be individual and his potentialities for taking those opportunities are the very consequence, not of his dependence on others, but of his interdependence with others.

The moralizers have quite rightly emphasized the importance of the individual's commitment to values and of the need for greater individual sense of responsibility. Although they have, in my opinion, misinterpreted why these qualities are needed and how they are to be brought about, they have had the positive effect of combatting an evasion of recognition of the demands on personality. On the other hand, they have perhaps performed a disservice in their resistance to the necessity of complex social interaction. Such distortion, however, may be salutary, in that sometimes all issues cannot be faced at once, for they would prove too threatening. Since the necessity for interaction in more complex social organization is already deeply entrenched, concentration on human effort—at the present, a more problematical factor—is perhaps the preferable focus, if one is going to be selective.

The reformers—although more concerned about the workings of social organization—have so distorted the picture of American society that they cannot be said to enrich available knowledge directly. There is, however, an important exception. In focussing on the issues of lost identity and self-alienation, they have struck a resonant chord in many readers who—in facing the strains we have talked about—thoughtfully seek answers among those pages that undeniably display a deep concern with the problems of finding meaningful human ties in modern society. What they read there is often their first introduction to the complexities of society and the nature of its organization. Many go on to further investigation and broaden the base of their newly found knowledge.

In summary, *insofar as* the two ideological points of view may have *positive* consequences, the moralizers' emphasis on individual commitments serves to generate the resources of personality, which—in terms of the current strain—are crucial. The reformers' emphasis on social conditions serves to increase, however indirectly, an understanding of the nature of society and of the reasons underlying the demand for personality development.

Finally, both may bring about new normative definitions of situations which members of the society are facing for the first time, situations that are at present characterized by uncertainty, or anomie. Although ideologies tend to confuse normative and empirical definitions of situations, they may effect a distinction between the two. That is to say, what "ought to be done" is distinguished from the conditions in which action is carried out, conditions that involve considerations other than simply implementing the desirable.

The point of view this book has taken may be accused of having addressed itself to discussing an "ideal system" and of having been insufficiently concerned with the empirical failures to live up to that ideal. Apart from the problem of interpreting the slim data as to what are failures and what are not, no discussion of change and of emerging patterns can be carried out solely on the basis of particular raw data, often ideologically perceived.

My position throughout has been that the changes of the past could give us a clue to the nature of future changes, and that emerging normative patterns raise the level of order in the society. In doing this, these new normative patterns raise the level of what is expected of people in the society in advance of their ability to fulfill these expectations. The process of what I have called upgrading has, it seems to me, been effected by such a leverage exerted on man. Indeed, many of the alleged failures are a result of feelings of relative deprivation as expectations rise faster than man is able to fulfill them.

Those who agree with my interpretation of this process might well point out that man's ability to fulfill these expectations is being forced too fast. Just as the infant cannot be forced too far in advance of natural rates of maturation without disaster, so—they might suggest—higher expectations with all their upgraded demands are asking too much of man too soon. But progress, and I call it that quite unabashedly, has never been gained without cost. How much the cost will be, it is too early to tell. In any case, the question of paying the cost for further gains has not been the ideological issue concerning us. The question is the intellectuals' contention that deterioration and loss, not gains, characterize the human condition in American society.

One eventuality seems reasonably certain. No "end-of-the-line" has been reached in American society; its economic maturity does not herald the cessation of further development. Nor does its talent for political compromise herald the end of ideology, for ideology may be concerned with other than political issues. Further—and more difficult—stages of growth face the society, and ideologists will continue to serve by calling attention to pressing problems and mobilizing the resources of society to face them.

The Role of the Intellectuals

9

The Intellectuals' Perception
of Strain

Although we have conceived of ideology as a reaction to strain, we cannot predict the nature of that reaction solely from the knowledge of strain itself. The formulation of an ideology depends on who is reacting and how he perceives the strain. In this chapter we will examine the relationship between strain and the ideological reaction to it. We are fortunate in having two types of reaction as a basis for comparison.

When the intellectuals tell us that the individual in American society is either too willing to conform or is forced to conform, they are telling us what *they* think individuals are doing. We have already dealt with the extent to which we think their imputations are justified. We have assessed the validity of their statements by asking whether individuals are actually conforming too much. Now we are asking why the intellectuals have made these particular statements instead of some others. If our analysis of strain is correct, why did the intellectuals, instead of making the same analysis as ours, interpret individual behavior as overconformity? Why have they overlooked, or denied, what we consider to be the principle source of strain? What we are looking for is the connection between strain, the demands for personality development, and the ideological reaction to it, the imputation of overconformity. The link between them is to be found in the way the intellectuals perceive strain.

Psychological Parallels

The following discussion will proceed on the assumption that some of the social processes in ideological reaction have an analytical resemblance to certain psychological processes. The patterns of analysis that clinical psychology, particularly Freudian psychology, has developed in the study of personality provide us with a useful scheme for analyzing comparable processes in the society. The assumption is that the *patterns* of relationships among structural parts in each case are parallel, although the actual structures involved are, of course, different. We are generalizing from the more familiar psychological patterns in applying them to another range of phenomena. This does not imply, however, that the analysis of social processes does not have to be carried out independently, that it can simply be derived from studying psychological phenomena alone.

Since knowledge about these psychological processes preceded that of comparable social processes in the development of social science, we will, when necessary, extend the psychological terminology already available. But it must be understood that we are not using psychological terms to discuss the *internal* functioning of the personality but are applying them to the society in ways to be specified.

For the purposes at hand, there are two analytical resemblances: 1) between psychological defense mechanisms and the ideological reaction to strain; and 2) between the socialization of the child and the mechanisms of social control in general.

Ideology as Defense Mechanism.—Ideological perception of strain is by definition selective and distorted. The way in which that perception screens out certain aspects of the situation and distorts others can be compared to the psychological defense mechanisms of personality. Just as the individual's ego reacts to anxiety by falsifying and distorting reality in order to avert a threat, an ideological reaction acts to protect the society, or groups within it, from some threatening aspect arising from social strain.

An ideological definition of the situation can be analyzed as an attempt to interpret strain in such a way that its threatening aspects may be evaded. The interpretation may utilize the defense mechanism of *denial*: it claims there "really" is no strain at all. Or it may resort to the mechanism of *displacement*: it avoids facing the actual source of strain by claiming that the threat arises from some other source, when in fact it does not. Another defense mechanism we have already discussed is *regression*: the wish to return to earlier phases of development in order to avoid the threats and frustrations of the present stage and to attain the satisfactions of the earlier stage. We will apply these concepts and a few others to be defined.

Demands and Support in Social Control.—The socialization of the child by his parents is characterized by patterns that can be applied to the control of the individual by society. Actually, it is not true that society acts *in loco parentis* but that parents act as "intermediate agents of control" over children for the society. Just as parents teach the child what is expected of him and restrain him from unacceptable behavior, so society reinforces the individual's commitment to do what is expected of him and checks his deviant tendencies. For the sake of simplicity in discussion, I will deliberately personify "society" as if it were an agent "doing" this and "expecting" that. This is meant to be a synecdochic short cut to refer to other people with whom the individual interacts. The reinforcements and restraints of society are not entirely external. In childhood the expectations of society become internalized (Freud's superego), and "conscience" becomes a constant reminder of society's demands. Thus the individual, broadly speaking, learns to expect of himself what society expects of him.

In Chapter 8, we pointed out that the current strain poses the problem of maintaining a balance between demands for performance and the need for emotional support. Society demands performance from the individual, and the individual personality needs emotional support—love, approval, security, etc.—from society.

In the family, the mother is the primary source of emotional support. It is she who is mainly concerned with the child's nurturance and with gratifying his needs for dependence. Although she is largely responsible for training the child and teaching him new levels of performance in infancy, the father is the primary model in setting for the child what is expected of him in the larger society, particularly since the father's occupational role and the standard of living he provides his family are the chief determinants of the entire family's status.

Particular families, of course, may vary from this pattern with respect to which parent, or even occasionally other relatives or parent-surrogate, performs which function. But unless both functions are fulfilled, the child is likely to experience serious personality disturbances.

The society may be said to fulfill parallel functions for the individual. The values of the society, like the father in the family, are a model in that they set standards for desirable levels of performance. A traditional society with a subsistence economy, for example, demands considerably less of its members than a highly industrialized society. The values of American society expect its members to make something of themselves, "get ahead," and seize the opportunities that are available. With the changes we have noted, the expected levels of performance have risen. However these expectations may impinge on different persons in different roles, the society is demanding higher levels of performance of its members in general.

Conversely, the society must also give support to the individual by rewarding him and approving of him in terms of his performance. The nature of the rewards and approval is not relevant here (be they income, status, prestige, or whatever), nor is the nature of the valued performance.

The essential point, for our purposes, is that if there is a serious imbalance between demands and support, strain will ensue. The intellectuals' perception of strain clearly implies that they consider the source of strain to be this imbalance between social demands and social support. Let us review their positions with this in mind. We shall see that their perception of the imbalance is related to their notions about the nature of man and his relation to society.

The Moralizers' Perception of Strain

The moralizers assume that social conditions are shaped by individual responsibility for affirming values. They assert that the individual has abdicated this responsibility to the group. Because of slackness of character, he has virtually given up steering his own course and has turned to others for direction. Since most of the others are doing the same thing, hardly anyone is making a constructive impact on social conditions, which are said to depend on individual leadership. It is as if everyone were gathering around the drinking fountain and no one were minding the store. An alleged lack of leadership implies that there is a *deficit of power*. In a section entitled "Who has the power?" (1950, pp. 242-55), Riesman says that the new-style other-directed business leader may pound the table, but he looks to others for leadership and does not care to get out of line with his peer-group. There is an "indeterminacy and amorphousness in the power situation" (p. 255).

According to this interpretation, social participation has increased because the individual has rushed into social inter-action *for security and support* instead of "standing on his own feet." This is why he (or she) stampedes in herds to community meetings, to church, cocktail parties, *kaffee-klatsches*—to group activities in general.

In the business firm and at the university, executive and professor alike are criticized for working in groups instead

of thinking for themselves and assuming the responsibility
for their own decisions. They flock to the conference table
for reassurance and approval, encouraged to do so by the
facile "scientism" of "group dynamics." Similarly, parents
abdicate their responsibility for rearing children by packing
them off to organized group activities—preschool nurseries,
scout meetings, and the like.

The moralizers explain this abdication of responsibility
by linking it to the real increases in functional capacity of
the society, which they interpret as preponderantly scientific,
technological, and economic. We have already examined the
intellectuals' comments on the misapplication of science
(pseudo, as in the case of Whyte's "scientism," or otherwise): the individual evades the more difficult moral decisions in favor of applying the less equivocal standards of
science, even in dealing with other persons. In discussing
occupational roles, Max Lerner for example, refers to the
"Neutral Technician," who is characterized by a kind of
nihilism of values along with an exaltation of techniques
(1957, p. 236).

In the technological and economic area, the moralizers
propose that these functions have become so efficiently
organized that society does for the individual what he formerly had to do for himself; the hard work, saving, and bearing
of risk that formerly fell on the individual is now, as Riesman
put it, built into the system. With the attainment of a mature
economy, an end-of-the-line in development has been reached.
In terms of a Toynbee-like challenge-and-response formulation, the challenge to the individual has been removed now
that the goals that previously directed him from within himself have become unnecessary. Now they are automatically
attained by the system. Without challenge, the individual
—like Toynbee's civilizations—regresses.

In terms of the balance between demands and support,
the moralizers' verdict is that a serious imbalance prevails:
*as demands for performance decline, the need for support
becomes unrestrained and excessive.* Their emphasis on in-

dividual responsibility leads them *to evaluate positively the demand side and to evaluate negatively the support side.*

To draw on our analogy with the family, this type of imbalance would prevail if the father were failing to perform his function. Without the father, the child is in search of an author; he gropes for identity and becomes increasingly dependent on the mother. This increased dependency on mother with its seeking for earlier satisfactions is a form of regression. That is to say, if the needs for support and security are not restrained by the parents, especially by the father, regression occurs.

The relation between the individual and society, although admittedly more complex, is analytically parallel. Society must restrain the regressive needs for support of its members so that their capacities for performance may be developed and utilized. To paraphrase Freud (1955), human life has a twofold foundation in work and love, but love must be kept within limits if work is to be done.

The moralizers, therefore, interpret the current situation as a regression resulting from the decline of such restraints: "We are going soft." With increasing economic affluence and social (inter)dependence, people flock to the "market" to satisfy hedonistic wants, buying consumer goods they do not "really" need. They flock to groups for emotional support. They turn *en masse* to mass culture for regressive distraction. To put it symbolically, with father gone, they rush to mother's breast. There has been a breakdown in social control.

Parsons' paradigm of social control (1951, p. 322) describes this kind of breakdown as seduction. Individual abdication of responsibility is interpreted by the moralizers as *seduction of the individual by society.* It is, of course, possible for such a state of affairs to exist. But if it were true to the extent alleged, the disruptions in the social order would be much more serious than they are.

Despite the part played by social conditions in this analysis, it must be remembered that the moralizers do not believe that the alleged unsatisfactory state of affairs can be blamed on those conditions. Where seduction is concerned, there is always a sufficient number of temptresses around. The individual is morally responsible for resisting them. In this way, the liberal hope, as Reinhold Niebuhr put it, will be attained and "all social institutions will gradually become the bearers of a universal human will" (1952, p. 68). In religious terms, the individual must prove by his performance that he is in a state of grace; by his performance, his moral heroism, he can help build God's kingdom on earth.

The Reformers' Perception of Strain

The reformers stand the moralizers' interpretation on its head. Given the proper conditions, they say, man is essentially good. It is senseless to talk about his responsibility when unfavorable conditions preclude the possibility of his making a choice. With the emphasis on real factors, this approach interprets the increasing social (inter)dependence in predominantly political terms. In a Hobbesian manner, it analyzes society (at least, non-utopian society) in terms of a distribution of power.

Moreover, they share the Marxian tendency to subsume economic factors under the political: any particular economic arrangement entails one, and only one, political way of life. Because they make this assumption, the apprehension that they share with the moralizers about the overemphasis on economic productivity and consumers' goods tends to be interpreted as a *political* feature of the society.

The key to this approach is *alienation*—starting with the alienation of labor in capitalism and proceeding to the dissolution of community ties, resulting in man's alienation from himself. Alienation (what we call increasing structural differentiation) has allegedly taken from man the power to choose for himself what he wants to do and when. With the increasing complexity of social organization that this process entails, he is more and more dependent not only on decisions made by others but by the very operation of the system itself. When the "system" takes over, power becomes anonymous. Even those at the "top" (except perhaps Mills' alleged power elite) are trapped in the system. Power is conceived of in zero-sum terms: the more it gets built into the system (the politically overorganized bureaucracy), the less it remains in the hands of individuals. Thus we end with what Heinemann called "institutional alienation": human institutions become impersonal and anonymous.

As the moralizers also contend, the increases in functional capacity have been attained at too high a cost. But the interpretation is again the reverse. Man has himself become "instrumentalized" in the process; the process of rationalization has swept him along with other factors of production as another calculable means. He, too, is now a commodity on the market—not just on the labor market, but on the "interpersonal" market as well. With the dissolution of community ties that informed one of who and what the "others" were, meaningful standards of relating to others have been effaced. In modern society, man has lost the direction these standards supplied and is increasingly dependent on others. Since the others are similarly alienated, the source of guidance becomes what Fromm calls "the anonymous *authority* [my italics] of public opinion and the market." Man experiences "an ever-increasing though mainly unconscious sense of powerlessness" (1955, p. 99). Again, power is transferred from the individual to the system. In the last analysis, power becomes the preponderant means of social control. The contrast with the moralizers' concern over the *deficit* of power is dramatic.

Thus, the data we reviewed are interpreted as evidence of increasing bureaucratic enslavement. On all fronts—at work and at the supermarket, in mass culture and in the crowded metropolis—the individual faces large organization. Deprived of allegedly saner standards, he is persuaded by the authority of the market in general and by advertising in particular to buy consumer goods. More wives and teen-age students are going to work to help pay the piper.

Like the moralizers, the reformers believe that the balance between demands for performance and needs for emotional support has broken down. But in this interpretation it is the support, not the demands, that has been withdrawn. With the emotional support of community ties gone, alienated man is powerless in a society dominated by anonymous authority. His relation to society is reduced to his being one of its instrumental means. To put it symbolically, he has been deserted by mother and faces the stark power of an authoritarian father without mother's support. Less metaphorically, he is *powerless* to resist social conditions.

As support by the society declines, the demands for performance become excessive. The emphasis on favorable social conditions for nurturing man's development and the assumption that man is essentially good lead to *a positive evaluation of the support side and a negative evaluation of the demand side.*

The reformers thus see conformity as a *compulsive enforcement,* to use Parsons' term, by the anonymous authority of the group. The alienated, powerless individual is forced to conform. The moralizers see conformity as submitting to the *seduction* of the group—or, simply, going soft. The diagnosis in both cases, arrived at from opposite points of departure, is the same: American society is blighted by conformity and mass culture.

The reformers' cure is a reduction in alienation, a dedifferentiation of the social structure. In the explicitly Marxian formulation, this means restoring power to all men (symbolically through the Party) through joint participation in decision-making. In economic organization, it means combining the managers' and workers' functions. As Braybrooke (1958) points out, it does not advocate completely abolishing specialization, since this would necessitate a return to a subsistence economy. But it does entail a reduction in the division of labor so that each man will no longer be confined to a single skill but will have and exercise many skills, which will include at least one manual and one intellectual. Through joint participation in a society where all will work with both hands and head, "Work will be divided but men will not." Community will be restored.

Ambivalence and Defense Mechanisms

The intellectuals' have displaced strain from what we believe to be its source to an alleged imbalance between social demands and social support. Moreover, there are two intellectual interpretations, each one disagreeing with the other as to which way the balance is tipped. To analyze the dynamics underlying these perceptions, or what we believe to be misperceptions, some further understanding of the defense mechanisms involved is necessary.

When strain is introduced into a system—be it the family, some other group, or the entire society—an individual in that system is likely to feel resentment. Other people with whom he interacts are not living up to his expectations of them. They make him do things he does not want to do; they prevent him from doing things he would like to do; they may fail to gratify his need for support or frustrate him in other ways. Consequently, he feels resentment and a desire to withdraw from the relationship to escape its frustrations. At the same time, however, he has a need to retain the security and meaning that it provides. The harboring of these opposite feelings at the same time is *ambivalence*. It is, of course, most familiar in the case of loving and hating the same person.

Since it is a further source of anxiety for the individual to have at the same time two conflicting feelings about the same person (or persons), he will seek to protect himself from the conflict with various defense mechanisms. There are many complications involved in the ways in which ambivalence may be handled, but for our purposes we need consider only one relatively straightforward resolution of the problem.

First, one of the conflicting feelings, one side of the ambivalence, is repressed. *Repression* is a defense mechanism wherein a feeling is pushed into the individual's unconscious so that he does not have to admit, consciously, that he feels that way. The repressed feeling, however, does not vanish just because there is no awareness of it. It struggles for conscious expression, so to speak. If it does emerge into consciousness, the individual is once again faced with the conflict of his ambivalence. Therefore, in order to protect himself from this eventuality, he may strive to maintain and buttress the repression with the defense of *reaction formation*: the compulsive overassertion, or exaggeration of the conscious side of the ambivalence. Thus, if he feels both love and hate for the same person and represses his hate, he will compulsively overassert his love in order not to give in to his repressed wish to hate. He protests too much.

Finally, the individual may then relieve some of the pressure built up by repression by expressing it, or "taking it out," in such a way that the repressed feeling is deflected from conflicting with the conscious feeling. This deflection can be accomplished in two ways to be considered here. One is by *displacement*, which we have already discussed. Thus, if A is repressing his hatred for B, he may displace it by consciously feeling that he "really" hates C. The second defense in this respect is *projection*: imputing the repressed feeling itself to someone else. Here A claims that it is not *he* that feels hatred but that it is "really" B, or perhaps someone else, who hates. In displacement, the *object* of the repressed feeling is transferred; in projection, the *subject* is transferred.

We must now attempt to explain why the intellectuals' account of strain does not coincide with ours. The explanation will apply the psychological processes involved in ambivalence and its defense mechanisms to the ideological reaction to strain. In analyzing the intellectuals' interpretations, their assessment of what is wrong and what is to be done, I am analyzing the thought processes that led them to make their *interpretations* of behavior; I am not suggesting that they themselves are actually behaving in the manner to be described. That is beside the point and none of my concern.

It is perhaps significant to note that often many persons adhere intensely to ideological judgments of behavior that they largely ignore in their own actions with little awareness that the two do not coincide. Those, for example, who condemn working in groups and "depending" on others often in fact pursue such behavior. Those who claim that modern man is alienated and oppressed by society give no evidence of being alienated and oppressed themselves. It is a felicitous irony, from the observer's point of view, that sometimes a person's behavior, whether he is aware of what he is actually doing or not, can be more constructive than his beliefs about that type of behavior. Such a person, however, will be convinced that his beliefs about what behavior should be are superior to his actual behavior. Fortunately, people do not always act on the basis of their professed social "theories"; they just interpret what they *think* they are doing.

One more caution. In distinguishing between the two types of ideologies, I have based the perception of strain that each subscribes to on the ideas each has about the nature of man and his relation to society. I am not, however, prepared to state which particular persons or social types of persons in American society subscribe, or are likely to subscribe, to either of the two ideologies. That problem—important though it may be—is beyond the scope of this book.

Strain and Stages of Development

Increasing complexity in the society has resulted in a greater differentiation of roles for members of the society. These newly differentiated roles must be co-ordinated—by the group for the interaction among several persons, and by the individual of the several roles he plays. Emancipation from previous forms of ascription has resulted in an increased capacity for performance with an upgrading of demands and an increase in the number of choices to be made. Individuals are confronted with the problems of meeting the greater demands and of defining the standards by which new choices are to be made.

All of these consequences, which we have spelled out in detail, are what we mean by greater demands for personality development. These demands can be said to characterize a new stage of development in American society. In Chapter 8, we noted that both Riesman and Rostow, for example, agree that the society is in (or is entering) a stage qualitatively different from the preceding stage of economic development. We differed from their interpretation in suggesting that the new stage is characterized by higher levels of performance and demands for performance.

We shall speak, therefore, of "higher level" as representing the current (or emerging) stage and of "lower level" as representing any previous stage; "higher" will mean more complex, more differentiated, and "lower" will mean less complex and less differentiated. Thus, we speak of man as a "higher" form of life than the ape.

The current strain of greater demands causes members of the society to feel anxiety about their ability to meet those demands. This anxiety may then lead to ambivalence: individuals will feel a positive desire to meet the demands and a negative one to evade them. The two types of ideological thought resolve this ambivalence in opposite ways. Each resolution is related to the perception of strain, which in turn was shaped by beliefs about "individual responsibility" on the one hand and "favorable social conditions" on the other.

The Moralizers' Interpretation of Behavior

In terms of the moralizers' positive evaluation of the demand side of the demand-support balance, the individual asserts the wish to meet the demands and represses the wish to evade them. He also represses the wish that the demands be withdrawn so that he does not have to face them at all. The latter wish is consciously experienced as a fear that perhaps the demands *have* been withdrawn ("things are too easy now"), thus allowing the situation to get out of control ("we're going soft"; "who has the power?"). If the demands are believed to be withdrawn, then one is left unprotected from his own regressive impulsives—hence, the negative emphasis on support. There is the danger of seduction.

In order to protect himself from giving in to his repressed wish to evade the demands, the individual overasserts, by means of a reaction-formation, his wish to meet the demands. He compulsively desires to perform adequately. But the evidence shows that he perceives adequate performance in terms of the previous stage of development in the society. He has a lower-level definition of adequate performance as independent action, avoiding reliance on groups and other people, etc. His reference is to what has been learned from the past and already understood.

If one leans over backwards to do what is expected of him (as defined at lower levels), then one will be able to resist the danger of seduction. Nor can *more* be expected of him in view of such exemplary behavior. In this way, the necessity of meeting greater demands on the higher level may be unconsciously evaded. The existence of the demands as such is denied. The individual succeeds in protecting himself from the threat of strain while still asserting that he wants to do what is expected of him. This phenomenon is common enough in the development of the child, for example, where the child resists efforts to teach him to achieve on higher levels by being compulsively "good" on lower levels. The defense employed here is regression, the attempt to remain at a lower stage of development where the demands are fewer.

The wish to evade higher-level demands for performance, such as the necessity for greater *inter*dependence with other people for example, is repressed. The "independent" responsibility of the lower level—"the good old days"—is compulsively asserted. Therefore, when other people do, in fact, perform at higher levels, their performance is interpreted in lower-level terms. Willingness to assume the burdens of greater interdependence, for example, is negatively evaluated as evasion of independent rugged individualism, thus allowing our hypothetical individual to project on to other people his own repressed wish to evade demands. When the wish to evade responsibility is imputed to others, he can consciously condemn the wish without condemning himself.

The Reformers' Interpretation of Behavior

Since the reformers' interpretation emphasizes positively the need for support but views the source of strain in terms of demands, their interpretation of strain is not a simple reversal of the moralizers' one. There is a reversal in that, with the negative evaluation of demands, the wish to meet the demands is repressed and the wish to evade them is asserted. But before we can justify that statement, we must first consider the reformers' emphasis on the need for support because of its importance in this syndrome.

The individual has a strong need to be approved of and accepted by society. But since the society the individual lives in is a society where support is contingent on fulfilling demands, meeting the greater demands generates anxiety in that if he fails to perform adequately, he will lose his support. This may lead to the unconscious fear that he is not worthy of support, that he is, so to speak, "unlovable." The latter fear is consciously experienced as a fear that support *has* been withdrawn and that he has been rejected by the society (as in "loss of communty ties," "alienation of man"). If he believes that support has been withdrawn, then he is left alone to face the hostile demands of an authoritarian society.

Without emotional support, the individual's anxiety about attaining higher levels of performance becomes acute. Without rewards, he feels there is no use in trying because he would not get anything for it if he did. What could be less rewarding than a demanding society where the source of the demands, that is, authority, is *anonymous*? Therefore the individual feels that the demands are unreasonable and that they are being enforced on him. He experiences an overwhelming preoccupation with power and authority.

The individual consequently represses any wish to meet those demands. In order to protect himself from giving in to this wish, he overasserts his wish to evade them. He seeks to be independent of the threatening relationship. Because of the repressed fear that he might allow himself to be dominated—that is, do what is expected of him—his independence becomes compulsive (the reaction formation). The compulsive independence is then rationalized as "autonomy," nonconformism, and the like. He will depend on himself and "go it alone." Thus he has *also repressed his wish for support*.

With the emphasis on "independence," the efforts of others to perform on higher levels is negatively evaluated as a submission to compulsive enforcement. The individual sees these efforts of others to achieve interdependence on higher-level terms as giving in to unreasonable demands, thus allowing him to project his own repressed fear of being dominated on to others. Since his repressed wish for support is particularly strong, he also projects it by claiming that others "market their personalities" for approval. They sell themselves for love, if you will.

Two Horror Novels

The two horror novels of future society, *Brave New World* and *1984*, might be looked at as projections of these two ideological points of view. The fears that would allegedly be calmed by the utopia of a romanticized past become frighteningly alive in these caricatures of future societies.

Huxley's *Brave New World* depicts a society where the dire prophecies of the moralizing humanist come true. The transcendent values of nobility, heroism, and self-denial have become obsolescent and "built into" the system. As Mustapha Mond tells John, the Savage:

> But industrial civilization is only possible when there is no self-denial . . . civilization has absolutely no need of nobility or heroism. . . . In a perfectly organized society like ours, nobody has any opportunities for being noble or heroic. (1932, p. 161)

Shakespeare and the Bible—in short, the humanities—have been prohibited. The transcendent principle of technology has taken their place, apotheosized in the notion of Our Ford—the very symbol of industrial organization. The "new" Bible is *My Life And Work, By Our Ford*, published by the "Society for the Propagation of Fordian Knowledge" (p. 148)—Huxley's shrewd anticipation of the fear that Foundations, as organizations, would replace individual effort. Mustapha Mond ("must have a world"?) is the Resident World Controller for Western Europe, the archetypal Madison-Avenue type manipulator who decides what is "best" for the public.

The *Brave New World* becomes a negative representation of Marcuse's fondest dream, at least in the sense that the system takes care of demands for performance so that individuals can afford to escape "surplus-repression" and regress to libidinous relationships. Free love and sensory gratification prevail. And capping the hedonistic abandon available through consumers goods, television, and the feelies is *soma,* itself the very agent of seduction by which the individual may evade reality and regress to a womb-like oceanic feeling.

In the scene where Lenina fails to seduce John, we see sex, the prototypical seduction, symbolizing the seduction of society—designed to derail the inner-directed Savage from his gyroscopic path. He, however, will not take his reward until he has proved himself worthy of it and ends up flogging himself in an effort to impose on himself the discipline the society *fails* to. He has the fantasy of whipping the seductress

Lenina as he whips himself, for Lenina represents his own regressive impulses to give in to society.

The fear of seduction in the *Brave New World* is replaced by the fear of compulsive enforcement in the world of George Orwell's 1984. Instead of a surfeit of hedonism, it is a bleak, loveless world of ugliness, ill-health, and deprivation; the statement of the hedonistic has been reversed. There is the familar preoccupation with power. Society is collective power over men and the Party is its agent. Big Brother is indeed the anonymous authority since no one sees or meets him but all must submit to him.

But, as O'Brien tells Winston Smith, "You must love Big Brother. It is not enough to obey him; you must love him" (1949, p. 214). The fact that Orwell symbolized society as a Big *Brother* and emphasized that he must be loved as well as obeyed reflects, it seems to me, the reformers' emphasis on the aspect of security and support in the relationship between man and society. Orwell could have symbolized despotic authority as simply a "leader" demanding obedience, but love too is demanded.

Since one must sell oneself for love, the punitive and demanding father becomes an elder brother, who can demand (brotherly) love as well. The wish to view society as a community of primarily supportive relationships is thus projected into a hideous caricature. The evil lies not in seduction by woman (excessive dependence on support) but in domination by man (excessive demands of power). Since Winston's love for Julia—the natural and spontaneous love of man for woman—is stamped out, this natural need must be replaced by a forced love for anonymous authority and power.

Conclusion

The reformers recommend that these inhuman conditions be eliminated by a restoration of community ties where men will no longer be divided. With joint participation, competition and individious distinctions will be eliminated. This represents a regression to a social structure even *less* differentiated than that desired by the moralizers. To use Riesman's terms, moralizers implicitly want to regress to an inner-directed society, but the reformers implicitly want to regress to an idealized tradition-directed society.

Underlying this difference in the "scale of regression" are the differences we have previously pointed out in the assumptions each group makes about man and his relation to culture and to society. Since the reformers' assumptions are less differentiated (because culture—in its evaluative sense—is not differentiated but is reduced to the nature of man), they are more regressive.

In the idealized type of unalienated society that the reformers recommend, we can see that *there* love is restored and power eliminated. In the unalienated society, the demands on personality will be eliminated, for personality will no longer be a differentiated, or alienated, resource. With competition and invidious distinctions eliminated through joint participation ("men will no longer be divided"), there is no problem of success for some and failure for others: the problem of performance disappears altogether. And the problem of rewarding performances disappears as well: *love become unconditional.*

In the reformers' ideal world, there is no problem of maintaining a balance between demands for performance and need for support, for one is no longer contingent on the other with respect to each individual. The "balancing" is somehow effected at the community level—"from each according to his ability, to each according to his needs"—through what seems to be a version of the utilitarian natural identity of interests—though "organically" rather than economically defined. Thus we come full circle back to the utilitarian notion that human wants are given, with the "givenness" inherent in human nature. And finally, the personality problem of integrating many differentiated roles is gone because man is no longer highly specialized and fragmented: his wholeness has been restored.

In its extremer form, this ideology is—as Aron, among

others, has pointed out (1957, p. 149)—equivalent to a secularized theology. It is the chiliastic hope of restoring utopia on earth. In the Garden of Eden before man ate of the tree of knowledge of good and evil, sin was not problematical. The Fall was the first step in the long process of alienation. Man fell from grace and became alienated from God. In the idealized community, we are told, utopian social conditions will eliminate evil, for man is essentially good: everyone will be in a state of grace. But what is involved here is not the elimination of evil but the elimination of the *differentiation between good and evil.*

10

Intellectuals as Agents of Ideas

A few years ago a forum was held at the Museum of Modern Art in New York on "The role of the intellectual in modern society." The panel members were Granville Hicks, Clement Greenberg, W. H. Auden, and Robert Gorham Davis (Berger, 1957, pp. 281-82). Auden, it is reported, looked around him and commented that the panel members were literary men. Had the forum been held in the Middle Ages, Auden pointed out, the "panel members would have been mostly members of the clergy; in the sixteenth and seventeenth centuries . . . mostly natural scientists; in the twentieth century, we are mostly literary men."

In Chapter 1, we defined intellectuals as social critics who seek to confront *in toto* the emerging problems of their time. Auden's comment on what group of persons might be considered intellectuals from time to time suggests, in a general way, that there is a relationship between the nature of problems that emerge in any given period and the kind of intellectuals whose interests those problems will elicit. As society becomes more complex, each successive stage of development presents its particular type of problems, problems that have never been stated before and that require new kinds of knowledge about society. Because of their interest in problems as social critics, intellectuals act as agents of problem-statement and stimulate the investigation and development of the new kinds of knowledge required. In this way, they extend the interest in problems to new areas, to new fields of learning that will be able to deal with the type of problems at hand. Those who investigate them will specialize in subject matter that up to that time had not required special attention and thus had not yet been differentiated from a larger body of knowledge. From the latter they carve out a new specialty.

As the new specialty develops, it advances its interpretation of subject matter that had previously been considered the domain of the less differentiated body of knowledge. Thus, ideological conflict between older and newer claims is likely to ensue—as in religion "versus" science, heredity "versus" environment—until, with further advance of knowledge and sophistication of theory, some equitable division of labor is worked out between the rival claims to legitimacy.

The ideological focus then shifts again as newer problems arise, newer areas of learning emerge. Thus, this process of the "history of ideas" (the "ideal factors") is not completely independent of changes in the structure of society itself (the "real factors"). Nor is it completely the result of them, for social action is often taken on the basis of new knowledge. Witness the influence, for example, of Keynesian economics. There is a constant interplay, an interdependence, between the changes taking place in society and the ideas that have sought to interpret and shape them.

In this way, the relation between the development of society and the development of knowledge about society may be looked at in terms of the relation between *interest in problems* and *theoretical knowledge*. Ideology is a mechanism, a means of communication, that mediates between the two. It performs this mediation by treating both sides of the relationship at once as if they could not be differentiated from each other. That is to say, the development of theoretical knowledge is not seen as independent of a particular interest in problems but rather as a direct reflection of it. When the knowledge that ideology stimulates becomes sufficiently established in its own right and is able to shake off the selective biases of particular approaches, ideology dies of its own success. It brings about the very differentiation it had overlooked or oversimplified. In this sense, it can be said that "sometimes new truth rides into history upon the back of error" (Niebuhr, 1944, p. 75).

In the following, we will first very briefly look into the relation between the problems of a developing society and theoretical knowledge about it. Then we will investigate the frame of reference in terms of which problems are perceived and theories formulated.

Interest in Problems and Theoretical Knowledge

I have suggested that the relationship between these two components and the ensuing reorganization of ideas takes place in an ideological field. An analysis of this process helps to explain who the ideological contenders may be in any given stage of development of society. A highly cursory view of such stages may then throw some light on the contemporary scene.

H. Stuart Hughes notes that from the sixteenth century on, a new class of lay intellectuals differentiated itself from the clergy and challenged the church monopoly of intellectual life (1956, p. 318). This differentiation was, of course, associated with the Renaissance and the Reformation and their legitimation of secular inquiry that encouraged the rapid development of sciences in the seventeenth century.

Interest in political philosophy was, in turn, generated by the rise of the nation-state out of feudal units and signalled the emergence of the social sciences as a differentiated body of knowledge. Differentiation *within* the social sciences can be said to have been spearheaded by economic theory associated with the rise of mercantile capitalism and, later, industrialization. Parsons points out that:

. . . intellectually economic theory of varying kinds provided the terms for defining the character of that period. Schools of thought ranged from the most orthodox laissez-faire capitalism through varying shades of liberalism and reformism to radical socialism, eventually crystallizing in Marxism; but underlying all these views was a common set of assumptions about the critical character of "economic factors." (1959b, p. 553)

Parsons goes on to suggest that the economic era was succeeded by a psychological one, in which—insofar as ideological concerns are involved—the focus was related to the impact of industrialization on the individual. The psychological, particularly Freudian, preoccupation with the irrational challenged the notion of "economic man" making "rational decisions" as an interpretation of human behavior. But it subsequently "became apparent that the understanding of the complexities of our large-scale society and its 'mass' phenomena require more than analysis of individual conduct" (p. 553). Sociological analysis was required as well.

Sociology, then, has entered the ideological field in making its bid as an interpreter of contemporary experience. In doing so, it has challenged some of the claims of other specialties (psychology, economics, and political science) in pre-empting their subject matter to varying degrees.

The primary ideological focus, however, is not among these specialties but between sociology—as the newest specialty that lays claim to a broader knowledge of human behavior—and that large division of knowledge from which all specialties have carved much of their subject matter—the humanities. In addressing itself to the problems of social structure and process, particularly on a large scale, sociology is expropriating subject matter from the humanities in dealing with such questions as the relation of the individual to society, the values involved in such a relation, and the state of culture in general. As Parsons has commented:

Differentiation and specialization put a particular strain on one group of intellectuals, those who tend to regard themselves as guardians of "general culture." These intellectuals are above all the humanistically inclined, both inside and outside the colleges and universities . . . they have traditionally been the intellectual experts on things human, and have had to face the invasion of their fields by a whole new crop of more technical and more specialized disciplines that have appropriated parts of this area, notably the social and psychological sciences. (1959a, p. 494)

For some three centuries, then, science has increasingly claimed for its own that *aspect* of knowledge which falls within the empirical-rational frame of reference. Scientific investigation of that aspect is a functional specialization. In consequence, the humanities have become less inclusive in scope and have relinquished—at least where physical matter is concerned—those concerns to the scientist.

The Frame of Reference

Pertinent to the development of knowledge about society, and about human action in general, is the frame of reference in terms of which interests in problems are perceived and theories about them are formulated. Should a scientific frame of reference, for example, include knowledge of both the physical *and social* worlds? Within the latter, should a distinction be made between cultural patterns and social organization?

Some of the main influences on intellectual thought in this respect may be discovered in German idealistic philosophy. I will draw on Parsons' (1949) brilliant analysis of this background for my discussion. Although the intellectual background of the moralizers' and elitists' ideologies may have roots other than the German idealism to be discussed here, the latter had a most important influence on them in shaping their notions about human action in society. The other main wing of thought at the time was in the positivistic-utilitarian tradition, which—although it influenced economic and political thought—did not give to those humanistically inclined the sense of cultural pattern they sought as the foundation for their approach to the problem of assessing man's place in culture and society.

Since the elitists and moralizers emphasize the individual and the unique qualities of human action and react against what they consider a depersonalized social order and an over-rationalized, "disenchanted" world, they are very much in the vein of nineteenth-century romanticism, a set of attitudes that German idealism was central in forming. On the other side of our ideological fence, the relevance of German thought for Marxism with its influence on the reformers' beliefs is, of course, patently clear.

Our first concern is with the following question: Can human action be studied scientifically as is the physical world? Or is the quality of human action so radically unique as to exclude it from the scientific procedures of analysis and investigation? German philosophical thought, which Kant had been instrumental in shaping, largely answered the latter question in the affirmative by making a sharp distinction between the physical and human worlds.

Kant's dualism distinguished between the physical world of "natural phenomena," characterized by deterministic, causal relationships, and the world of ideas, characterized by the freedom of concrete uniqueness and individuality (Parsons, 1949, pp. 473-95). Knowledge, therefore, was conceived of as divided into two qualitatively different types, *Naturwissenschaft* (knowledge of "nature") and *Kulturwissenschaft* (knowledge of "culture"). The principles of analysis and procedures of investigation of one could not be applied to the other. While this dualism put the philosophical stamp of approval on the already established scientific investigation of the physical world, it also made knowledge of culture and of human action in general "safe" from the incursions of science.

In his discussion of these lines of development, Parsons points out that the study of man and of culture, thus excluded from the phenomenal, scientific sphere, generally was pursued in two directions. One was detailed, concrete history; the other was "philosophiz[ing] about these actions and events in terms of their significance for the totality of human development" (1949, p. 475). Hegel carried the latter conception further by arranging human actions in relation to a comprehensive cultural pattern, or *Geist*, under which individual acts were subsumed.

This view of cultural totality as a pattern was an organic

view, as opposed to the "mechanistic'" and "atomized" views
of the scientific thought that prevailed at the time and the
utilitarianism of social thought related to it. The term "organic" meant roughly the same thing as "patterned" and
emphasized what was considered the desirable quality of
"wholeness" in contrast to the undesirable qualities of "frag-
mentation" and "atomization."

This organic conception of a cultural totality is the intellectual ancestor of the elistist and moralizing ideologies.
This does not imply that the latter are necessarily Hegelian,
but rather that they embrace the notion that individual
action is a freely willed expression of cultural ideas and
they evaluate "wholeness" highly. With the rejection of
analytical or "mechanistic" explanations, the only generaliza-
tions one can make about action are statements about the
pattern of ideas itself.

The relationship between the pattern of ideas and individual acts is a complex one. Where the emphasis is on
the pattern, all human action is considered to be an expression of it; where some sort of Hegelian dialectic is absent,
the pattern is seen as relatively stable. This point of view
is familiar in anthropological studies of non-literate societies
—for example in the approach associated with Ruth Benedict—where each society is seen as a reflection of a unique
pattern. It is also familiar in the elitist view that certain
classes and regions are expressions of folk culture.

The Hegelian approach introduces the notion of a dynamic
force as an "emanation" of stages of "self-realization" of
the pattern (Parsons, 1949, p. 479). In the elitist version,
however, this dynamic force resides in the elite as agents
of the culture itself. They preserve its pattern, add to it, and
transmit it. The elitists then, place greater emphasis on
individual action, freely willed, although it is still not random
action, for only those who belong in a particular place in
the pattern can represent it authentically and act as its true
agents. In at least this sense, the evolution of the pattern
is still contained within itself.

The moralizers' ideology is a more radical break with

the notion that the pattern is self-realizing, for its preservation, enrichment, and transmission are carried on by agents
not identifiable within the pattern itself. With the expectation that all men may become "elite" if they but try and
are found worthy, the pattern itself is more subject to
change and more dependent on the commitments and contributions of individuals to it. The emphasis on concrete
uniqueness and individuality, however, is even stronger than
in the elitist version. The moralizers see a direct relationship
between the individual and his cultural pattern and reject
the notion that any intervening factors—such as social organization—have any determining influence.

The aversion to social science (once it begins to emerge),
which would introduce such intervening factors for consideration, is particularly strong—not only because it invades
an area of knowledge long considered the eminent domain
of the humanities but because in so doing, it makes assumptions about human action that seemingly undermine established premises. Durkheim pointed this out seventy years ago:

The same antagonism breaks out each time a new science is
founded. . . . But it is especially when man became an object of
science that the resistance became fierce. The believer, indeed, cannot but find repugnant the idea that man is to be studied as a
natural being, analogous to others, and moral facts as facts of nature.
It is well known how these collective sentiments, under the different
forms they have taken, have hindered the development of psychology
and sociology. (1949, pp. 285-86)

Perhaps part of this resistance is due to the misunder-
standing that arises from conceiving of social science as
"mechanistic," as a body of knowledge that presumes to
predict all concrete, individual behavior in cause-and-effect
terms. Social science, as an *analytical* body of knowledge,
does make statements and predictions about certain aspects
of human behavior within defined ranges. In doing so, it is
asserting that behavior is not random, that not just "anything" can happen. In asserting this, it is probably no more
deterministic than some humanistic notions about "innate
character," "temperament," "family traits," and the like,

not to mention their notions about the characteristics of classes and regions!

Rather than view the knowledge that social science may make available as a devaluation of human autonomy, one may indeed regard it as enhancing it.

Hence the paradox . . . the opportunity for relative emancipation from social determination increases proportionately with insight into this determination. (Mannheim, 1936, pp. 47-48)

Or, as Engels simply put it, "Freedom is the knowledge of necessity."

In the study of *human action*, perhaps the first major differentiation in Western thought was that between ideal factors and real factors—a partly ideological, partly philosophical cleavage that, as our present material has shown, is far from having been resolved (at least at certain levels of intellectual discourse). For Hegel and others, human action was determined by ideal factors—the *cultural* pattern of ideas, beliefs, forms, and values. But for Marx, who broke with this notion, the dynamic force that shapes action is not in a cultural reference but in a *particular form of social organization*—what we have broadly referred to as structure.

Marx's focus, of course, was on the power-relationships (the "real" factors) that were rooted in the conditions of production. "Reason" was replaced by "class interests." Man, however, acted rationally by following his interests, as defined by social conditions. Any individual—whether exploiter or exploited—*had* to act in accordance with such conditions. "Once the individuals in [the system] are placed in the situations that are given, their actions are 'determined' so as to maintain the system [and] drive it forward in the evolutionary course . . ." (Parsons, 1949, p. 492).

In the Marxian emphasis on social conditions as the determinants not only of individual action but of ideological beliefs as well (the Marxian equivalent of "culture"), we see the main intellectual ancestor of the reformers' ideology with all the implications for their formulae for eliminating unfavorable conditions and the power-relations rooted in them. It is essential to note, however, that this point of view—with its preoccupation with the means and conditions of action—shoves the independence of culture into the background and ends up, in this respect, by assuming that ultimate ends are given in human nature.

This emphasis on real factors is a sort of "sociological imperialism," an attempt to explain all human action in terms of social conditions. Hand in hand with such explanation went the value-judgment of what social conditions ought to be. In reacting to the strains of industrialization, the Marxian conception of "desirable" social conditions was based not only on the simpler society of past times but also on the intellectual reference to "organicism" that Marxian thought had taken over from Hegelian thought. The desirable society was the idealized organic community (what Tönnies called *Gemeinschaft*). And this point of view permeated the German sociological thought, what Shils (1957) refers to as the German sociological romanticism of the time.

To return to the elitists and the moralizers, although they also deplore the loss of an "organic" totality, they are not concerned with the loss of community so much as with the loss of a prior cultural unity. Their emphasis on a comprehensive cultural pattern is one from which ideas about social organization have not been differentiated. They do not consider social organization as a set of factors that exerts an independent force on human action but rather as an expression of the general cultural pattern: it either fits the pattern or it doesn't. If it does not, it is to be resisted as a deviation in the same way that other deviations—such as individual irresponsibility, materialism, groupism, or behavioral science—are to be resisted.

Both ideological types, value-oriented and structure-oriented alike, derive their notions of what society ought to be like from social theories that not only oppose further differentiation of social structure but postulate the restoration of a "lost wholeness" by means of a dedifferentiation. Each of these types sees only one set of factors as causal and regards the other as a dependent consequence. Sociological theory today, we have insisted throughout, regards both ideal factors and real factors as analytically independent of one another: each set is a necessary condition, but neither is sufficient by itself.

In the preceding analysis, we have focussed our attention on the influence of previous "social theories" on contemporary intellectual thought. We have looked at the role of the intellectuals, so to speak, in terms of the legacy of ideas they have inherited and work with. Another aspect of the role of the intellectuals is their status in the society: What power and prestige do they have? What is their economic status? What sorts of persons are recruited as intellectuals? What are their contacts with each other and with the rest of society?

In analyzing the intellectuals' role, these latter considerations are also, as an independent set of conditions, an important area of investigation. An analysis of them would be required for the complete picture. But since these considerations have received considerably more attention in American sociological analysis of the intellectuals than the intellectuals' relation to the development of ideas, I have deliberately emphasized the latter, as a consideration that has to some extent been neglected.

Parenthetically, it is interesting to note that much of American sociological analysis, in its concern with socio-economic status, occupational roles, veto-groups and the like, gives the same sort of emphasis to real factors that Marxian thought does, although admittedly with quite different assumptions and implications. I suspect that this emphasis is partly due not so much to any theoretical inclination but rather to the fact that such components are more readily measurable than are those of ideas, beliefs, and values. Thus, a justifiable concern with methodological techniques may unwittingly tend to bias theory. However important these real factors are, the equally important ideal factors should not be shoved into the background just because they are not "hard" data.

The Ideological Marketplace

Taking off from Auden's comment on who the intellectuals might be in any given period, we have looked at the relationship between their role as ideological agents and the various kinds of ideas that provide them with a frame of reference for theoretical knowledge about society. Beyond our immediate concern with the intellectuals, however, lies the problem of who any of the parties to ideological conflict might be, for they are not necessarily intellectuals. In view of previous formulations, such as the Marxian, about the nature of ideological conflict and what parts of the social structure become involved in it, some further comments addressed to this problem may help us to understand the dynamics of the ideological process more fully. Then we will be in a better position to assess the consequences of ideological action—both for our case in particular and for all cases in general.

The Agents of Ideology.—In our analytical approach we do not believe that strain always evokes conflict between interest groups. The Marxian conception of class conflict has had considerable influence on thinking in this area and has tended to oversimplify the whole problem by conceiving of society as an arena where interest groups compete with one another for limited resources and where their intellectual spokesmen advance justification for the claims of these groups. The Marxian interpretation seems to assume a direct one-to-one correspondence between the causal strain and the reaction to it; that is, each strain results in one, and only one, reaction.

The essential distinction we are making is that there are often many types of reaction to the same strain, that "class conflict" is only one of many possible reactions, and that there are many forms of strain that do not directly derive from class commitment in the Marxian sense. Even in those cases where class conflict does exist, there is no guarantee that it is a straightforward representation of strain, certainly that originating in class relations. Sutton *et al.*, for example, have pointed out that so-called interest groups do not necessarily act in terms of their own immediate interests. The business interests, for instance, oppose certain types of government spending that would substantially increase the demand for their products (1956, p. 13).

Since strain is not evenly distributed throughout the society, it will have different effects on various segments of the population. But, to repeat, these segments need not necessarily be classes (in the sense of an economically determined, completely cross-cutting stratification of the society) or even interest groups. The intellectual ideology this essay is concerned with is certainly a case in point. Although intellectuals in general are often thought of as occupying the same social position in the society, we have seen how two groups within this same position have presented two contrasting ideological interpretations—interpretations based on *opposite* assumptions. The fact that their *conclusions* seem to be more or less in agreement has obscured the differences in their reasoning. And these differences, I submit, cannot be derived solely from their social position, from their status as intellectuals *per se.*

Restraints on Ideological Cleavage.—Ideology may or may not have positive consequences for the society. Competition between ideologies tends to polarize issues and to force other parts of the system to take sides. When such conflict spreads, irrelevant issues frequently become involved, with the consequence of further distortion and selectivity, each side idealizing its position as the sole claim to "truth." Mitigating circumstances, however, tend to arrest this vicious circle and to resolve conflict (which is not to say that the conflict does not again arise at other points of strain).

In the first place, ideological conflict takes place within a common framework of cultural values. Parties to the conflict, however much they may defend or repudiate the status quo, usually agree on the basic meaning of "life on this earth"; if they did not, their division would be on a fundamentally religious basis. Within Western culture generally, there is a broad consensus on the positive evaluation of life on earth, on belief in the dignity of man, on individual freedom of choice, and on mastering the environment. I find myself in complete agreement with Coser (1956a) on this point, for he supports Simmel's assertion that "conflict usually takes place within a common universe of norms and rules [or what I would prefer to call cultural values]."

Thus ideologies as widely divergent as Marxism and the business creed assume that life on this earth is a "good thing"; both lay claim to recommending a type of society where the individual will be able to realize his potentialities and where his freedom of choice will not be unnecessarily restricted. These areas of consensus are so common to Western thought that other meanings of life on earth are not even considered as possible bases of evaluation. The differences among ideologies lie in their beliefs about the ways in which these desirable things may be attained in a going society and in their notions about the obstacles to attainment.

These differences, however, are not always a simple matter of disagreement about social institutions or the allocation of social resources. Underlying them are often, as we have seen, differences in ideas about the nature of society and man's relation to it. These ideas—often implicit—make up what we have called a social theory, or social philosophy, and it is the task of ideological analysis to make them explicit and to assess their selectivity. Despite these differences, these general assumptions still fall within the general framework of Western culture, as do the range of major religious beliefs that it accommodates.

In addition to this "supraconflict" consensus, there may also be a "subconflict" solidarity that prevents ideological schism from completely splitting the society open. Thus, whatever the composition of parties to ideological issues may be, the same people do not find themselves aligned against each other on all issues. They are, moreover, also members in common of local communities, of regions, of churches, and the like. The cleavages that divide them do not all cut through the population in the same way. The solidarities that make up the society crisscross each other in various ways. It should be pointed out that the organization of particular societies will vary on this dimension, with some societies manifesting considerably more rigid divisions and greater strain than others.

The analytical factors underlying this degree of over-all cleavage are largely historical in nature and related to the extent to which the society is differentiated and to how this differentiation came about. An illustration of crisscrossing solidarities is the American two-party system, where each party is a coalition of many interest groups, and where ideological issues are often fought out within the party (much to the despair of many European political theorists!).

These integrative features overlying and underlying ideological conflict make possible a marketplace, if you will, where ideological exchanges may take place without completely disrupting the society and where attempts at resolution may be effected. Following a Marxian line of thought, Coser points how classes constitute themselves through such conflict and become aware of their community of interests. But he adds that these " 'reciprocal repulsions' maintain a total social system by creating a balance between its various groups" (1956a, p. 34). Without limiting this notion to "classes," his statement points out how interest groups form associations (labor unions, trade associations, and the like) to represent them and how new procedural norms are developed for reconciling conflicting claims (such as arbitration, lobbying, etc.).

Beyond this and of utmost importance, it should be remembered that conflict is not solely based on conflicting *known* interests. It very frequently arises because of uncertainty as to what procedures ought to be followed at all. With the increasing complexity of society, situations arise in which existing norms fail to prescribe what ought to be done. This is precisely what is meant by *anomie*, an inadequate normative definition of the situation. A very familiar instance of this state of affairs is to be found in legal adjudication, where parties to a dispute find existing laws an inadequate guide to their actions and are, in effect, asking the courts to tell them what to do.

Similarly, ideologists confront new situations of increasing complexity where existing institutional arrangements and structural conditions fail to implement the values of the society. If I may stretch a metaphor, ideologists state the problems for the larger society, take sides on the issues involved, and "present them in the court" of the ideological marketplace. In some respects, perhaps intellectual spokesmen are lawyers for disputing parties writ large, seeking to carve definition out of uncertainty.

The Positive Consequences of Ideology.—In the preceding section we have worked through the consequences of ideology for the *society*. We have treated it as a mechanism that mediates between the values of the society and its changing structural conditions. At the beginning of this chapter, we also treated ideology as a mechanism, but in a different context. There we focussed on its mediation between interest in problems and *theoretical knowledge about* society. There we were concerned not so much with what was actually worked out in a particular society but with the development of new theoretical knowledge about societies in general. This latter context is *cultural*, since generalized knowledge is a part of the cultural heritage. We emphasized, for example, how ideological controversies stimulate the development of new fields of learning. Thus ideologists, as agents of problem-statement, wear two hats. They speak at two levels of discourse—social and cultural. In each instance, moreover, there are also the other, familiar two aspects involved: the *evaluative*—the interest in what kinds of questions ought to be asked or in what ought to be done, and the *empirical*—the existing conceptions of what is thought to be the actual state of knowledge or of affairs at the time. We can tabulate these relationships as follows:

	Evaluative	Empirical	Positive Consequence
Cultural	Interest in problems	Existing social theory	New theoretical knowledge about society
Social	Values of society	Existing structural conditions	New normative definitions

Ideologists perform their mediating function by oversimplifying these distinctions. They overlook not only the analytical independence between the evaluative and the empirical but also between the cultural and social contexts. At the social level, the moralizers see values as determining social conditions and the reformers see conditions as determining values. At the cultural level, both formulate their social theory in terms of their particular interest in problems. And since both conceive of "problems" as the pressing, practical issues of the society, neither considers the development of knowledge about society *for its own sake*, independently of problems, justified. Thus, both tend to overlook the distinction between the cultural and social contexts as well.

With their more or less sociological approach, the reformers believe that sociology should address itself to urgent social problems. In so doing, it will not only bring about meaning to the contemporary scene but will avoid the danger of spinning out theories that allegedly have little pertinence. They overlook the fact that the investigation and development of sociological theory even without immediate concern for practical problems may often prove more useful in ultimately solving them. The differentiation between pure and applied research that has somewhat painfully been fought out within the American physical sciences remains a debated issue in the social sciences. On the other hand, the moralizers, with their humanistic approach, are *ipso facto* opposed to the development of sociological knowledge, for they are reluctant to relinquish another area of human behavior to a specialized field, much less a scientific one.

It should be remembered, though, that ideologists are confronting issues in a changing society where these distinctions have not yet clearly emerged for the issues involved. In resisting the emerging distinctions, they polarize the situation so that further differentiation is either arrested or precipitated. With a highly differentiated society like ours where conflicting ideologies compete for legitimation and where other forces of change prevail, the result is likely to be in the direction of further differentiation. Thus we have the seeming paradox that the attempt to suppress differentiation serves to hasten its actualization. Ideology unwittingly brings this about by stimulating new knowledge and eliciting new normative definitions. It dies of its own success and the "case" is settled, although no particular adversary can be said to have won a clear-cut victory.

The Sequence of Ideological Issues.—As old issues are settled, ideology turns to the new issues that arise as the society changes and develops. Where previously we looked at the broad sweep of issues that societies have been concerned with in Western culture since the Middle Ages, we may now look more particularly at some of the more specific issues on the American scene. C. Wright Mills (1953), in discussing the role of the intellectual, has suggested four areas of interest in which intellectuals have been involved in the recent history of American society.

First, there was the muckraking period preceding World War I during which corruption in an expanding society was attacked, a period Mills characterizes as one of pragmatic liberalism. Second, was the period of "cultivated relaxation" of the twenties, during which the apolitical, esthetic, and literary revolt against bourgeois and provincial philistinism took place. Third, in the thirties, the intellectual acted as a political agent, with optimistic faith in man's rationality and as vanguard of the proletariat. Fourth, the post-World War

II period is what Mills describes as interest in personal tragedy and political failure of nerve, although I would define it as a concern with mass culture and conformity.

In addition, there are a range of ideological issues that American society has never had to face because they were "solved," so to speak, when the Republic was founded. Perhaps the most salient features were the absence of an established aristocracy, the separation of Church and State with the absence of (church) establishment, and the political enfranchisement of the individual from ascriptive ties (with that of women not becoming a problem until later and that of the negro still to be realized).

The muckraking stage represented an effort to upgrade moral standards during a period of rapid expansion when considerable innovation was required to meet a host of new problems. Such innovation, although it was undoubtedly characterized by corruption, could not be dismissed solely on those grounds, as Lincoln Steffens discovered in his investigations. The pressure of meeting new demands occurred in situations where normative procedures had not yet been clarified, and muckraking ideology served to help make such moral clarification possible.

I would suggest that we are now entering another such period of ideological muckraking with regard to normative standards at the so-called mass-culture level. As "cultural" criteria have become emancipated from previous ascription to class, region, and economic status, there is bound to be indeterminacy in standards of choice among them and indeterminacy in the ways in which they are "distributed" by mass media to the available market. The current concern with status-seeking and mass consumption is perhaps an ideological effort that will serve, however indirectly, to clarify normative standards in what is now to some extent an anomic situation.

However, the shift from the political problems of the thirties to the cultural problems of the fifties seems most relevant to the issues at hand. With regard to the problem of mass-culture, I have suggested that the apparent alliance of the "conservative" and "liberal" wings of ideological thought, which have tended to converge into an elitist interpretation, is related to the fact that the standards now being focussed on are those over which the intellectuals consider themselves to be the guardians. The issues have now moved into their private domain.

Whereas in the economic crisis of the thirties, the intellectuals could unite against the business interests as symbolized by Wall Street, today issues are said to be less clear-cut. In the "cultural" crisis of the fifties and in the search for a common enemy, the only interest-group accessible for attack seems to be the putative agents of mass-culture—the advertisers symbolized by Madison Avenue. Madison Avenue has replaced Wall Street as the common foe.

That some intellectuals themselves are not wholly satisfied with a line of battle so drawn is evident in their frequent complaints that there are no "real" issues, no movements or causes, no audience. For them, the "real" issue seems to be the lack of issues. In what they perceive to be an ideological vacuum, they are agents with nothing to sell. As Aron puts it, "The American intellectuals of today are in search of enemies" (1957, p. 233).

Reformers who have not gone over to the elitist line on mass culture still cling to the political issues of the thirties. Refusing to believe that the New Deal reforms of that period largely resolved those issues, they regard that belief as evidence of political apathy and a panglossing of the *status quo*. As all social phenomena are said to be basically political, so ideology is political, or it is nothing.

Without a movement to which [they] might address political ideas, intellectuals in due course cease to express such ideas and so in time, shifting their interests, they become indifferent. (Mills in *Partisan Review*, 1952b, p. 448)

Sometimes even *Dissent* finds nothing more to say on political issues. In an editorial foreword to the issue of Summer 1957, Lewis Coser apologizes, "The issue contains rather little on present-day power relations; but here we would simply refer the reader to our friend C. Wright Mills' *Power Elite*" (pp. 212-13).

Closely related to this concern over the loss of interest in issues and movements is the preoccupation of intellectuals with being independent of society. They conceive of their role as being in society but not of it so that they can criticize society without having to cater to it. They are, as Lasswell might say, afraid of being restricted by partial incorporation. The extent to which other intellectuals have become "institutionalized" by working for foundations, even universities, or—worse yet—advertising and public relations, is regarded as a possible "selling out." It is what Rahv refers to as the "embourgeoisement of the intelligentsia" (*Partisan Review*, 1952a, p. 306). Sometimes this loss of independence is interpreted directly in terms of the political reference:

Intellect has associated itself with power, perhaps as never before in history, and is now conceded to be in itself a kind of power . . . whenever [the intellectuals] become absorbed into the accredited institutions of society, they not only lose their traditional rebelliousness but to one extent or another *they cease to function as intellectuals*. (Howe, 1954b, pp. 11, 13)

This self-image of independence becomes compulsive when the intellectual posture vis-à-vis the society is conceived of in all-or-none terms. The proposition seems to be that "either you're for us or you're against us." Just as the tired businessman who, weary of coping with others over complex issues, turns to the Western on the telescreen where the lone individual confronts unambiguous evil, so the compulsively independent intellectual seeks the common enemy, the out-and-out cause. It is in the nature of the case that such unambiguous conflict is conceived of in terms of power. Martin Cronin has suggested that the self-image of such intellectuals

. . . obviously owes something to the Marxist revolutionary, whose example, however discredited, still influences the American intellectual, if only because, like a woman between marriages, he has not yet reorganized his life around a figure of superior power. (1958, p. 411)

What has been called with some degree of euphemism the intellectuals' "lover's quarrel" with America is, as I suggested in Chapter 9, characterized by considerable ambivalence: they both desire to be accepted and heeded and fear being accepted, or "taken in."

The moralizers, by and large, do not complain of a lack of interest in issues and movements. They, too, are concerned with maintaining their independence as monitors of the culture, but they do not conceive of exercising their role by repudiating the existing social structure. It is, rather, among the hard core of those who hark back to the political thirties and who insist that ideology must be political that the compulsion to be independent is most strong. They are the ones who "seem determined to coddle every eccentricity, to cherish every grievance, to inflame every sore spot and sharpen every rough edge, lest they find their discontent diminishing" (Hicks, 1956, p. 290). Thus they can protect themselves against being "taken in."

This type of intellectual has commented that others who have sold out by joining in the "American celebration" cannot endure having a small minority at variance with the alleged defense of the *status quo*. What is more important, it seems to me, is not the fact that they choose to dissent, but that they are unable to find relevant issues as grounds for dissent. It is essential that some part of the intellectual world should serve the function of gadfly and maintain its independence of conventional interpretations. But it would also seem desirable that, in so doing, it push the ideological frontier into the newly emerging problems so that new issues may be defined.

It seems inconceivable that, in a society as complex and confusing as ours, no problems can be found that will recruit interest, no movements started that will generate support, no issues discovered that will engage conflict. Such discovery, however, will perhaps require more sophistication about what is going on in the society than is being brought to bear by those intellectuals presently on the American scene who claim that ideology is moribund because no one is interested in fighting issues that died two decades ago. The broad political issues of the thirties are as dead for the radicals as they are for the right-wing reactionaries, despite the efforts of both to revive them. As their ranks dwindle, it is becoming an increasingly hard core that insists on refighting old issues instead of facing new ones. The intellectuals who have shifted their concern from "politics" to "culture and conformity" have at least moved on.

Conclusion

I am aware that many readers will claim that my position is itself ideological because it considers change in the form of increasing social complexity as a good thing, and regression, or return to a simpler society, as a bad thing. If, however, the analysis I have presented is correct, increasing complexity through structural differentiation can result in (and, for American society, has resulted in) greater mobilization of resources, increased capacity to pursue whatever goals are deemed desirable, and greater freedom of choice for more individuals.

Not all men consider these results desirable. But they are, I submit, considered desirable by those who share the values that American society embraces. In particular periods of our history, those who have formulated these values may have conceived of the good society as an agrarian democracy, an entrepreneurial economy, a land of rugged individualists, a land of ascetic hard workers, or whatever. But these particular conceptions are time-bound. American values conceive of the ideally good society as one that continually seeks to develop the capacities of all its members and to provide them with the opportunities for exercising those capacities. In terms of these high expectations, American society—however good it may be—is never good enough.

As for those who consider it the better course to return

to simpler days, or to reduce the degree of complexity in one way or another, I stand with C. P. Snow in saying that they must also be willing to sustain the restrictions of freedom of choice and of opportunity that such a regression entails. Present problems cannot be escaped by regressing without also relinquishing present gains.

Above all, I am most definitely not seeking to pangloss the status quo by claiming that there are no problems. Nor have I, as has been quite obvious, come up with answers to the problems that do exist. I have sought to define these problems in a different way than the intellectuals have. My main concern has been not to answer old questions but to ask new ones.

One more counter-argument remains. Other readers might agree that this process of increasing differentiation has indeed resulted in the gains I have claimed. But, they might say, why should we assume that the process will continue in the same way? Have we not at last reached the point of diminishing returns? No one can be sure of the answer to that question. But of one thing I am sure. That question has been asked in one form or another since the time of prehistoric man. There have always been those who are willing to concede that the innovations of the past are all well and good but who resist further change by insisting that the time to call a halt has at last arrived. We have come a long way, they say, but now we have gone far enough.

I don't believe it. Nor do those Americans who seek new goals among new choices. The uncertainty of direction may bewilder them, but they are not seduced by pleasure or oppressed by power.

References

Adlow, Elijah. 1955. "Teen-age Criminals," *Atlantic Monthly*, July, pp. 46-50.
American Scholar forum. 1951. "Changing Values in the Western World," Summer, pp. 341-58.
———. 1952a. "The Application of Scientific Method to the Study of Human Behavior," Spring, pp. 208-25.
———. 1952b. "The Social Scientists' Reply," Summer, pp. 356-61.
Anders, Gunther. 1956. "The World as Phantom and as Matrix," trans. by Norbert Guterman, *Dissent*, Winter, pp. 14-24.
Andrieux and Lignon. 1956. "Life in the Factory," trans. by Harriman Jones, *Dissent*, Winter, pp. 29-36.
Arendt, Hannah. 1950. "The Mob and the Elite," *Partisan Review*, November-December, pp. 808-19.
———. 1958. *The Human Condition*. Chicago: University of Chicago Press.
Arnold, G. L. 1955. "Collectivism Reconsidered," *Dissent*, Autumn, pp. 305-16.
Aron, Raymond. 1957. *The Opium of the Intellectuals*. Trans. by Terence Kilmartin. Garden City: Doubleday.
Barrett, William. 1951a. "What Existentialism Offers Modern Man," *Commentary*, July, pp. 17-23.
———. 1951b. "American Fiction and American Values," *Partisan Review*, November-December, pp. 681-90.
Barzun, Jacques. 1952. "Artist against Society: Some Articles of War," *Partisan Review*, January-February, pp. 60-77.
———. 1954. "America at Play," *Atlantic Monthly*, February, pp. 38-41.
Bates, Marston. 1956. "The Discipline Trap," *American Scholar*, Autumn, pp. 459-67.
Bauer, Raymond A., and Alice H. Bauer. 1961. "American Society and the Mass Media of Communication," *Journal of Social Issues*. To be published.

Bell, Daniel. 1956. "The Theory of Mass Society," *Commentary*, July, pp. 75-83.

———. 1960. *The End of Ideology*. Glencoe: The Free Press.

Bendix, Reinhard. 1951. "The Image of Man in the Social Sciences," *Commentary*, February, pp. 187-92.

Benedict, Ruth. 1955. "Continuities and Discontinuities in Cultural Conditioning," in *Personality in Nature, Society, and Culture*, ed. by Clyde Kluckhohn and Henry A. Murray. 2nd ed. New York: Knopf.

Bentley, Eric. 1949. "A Note on American Culture," *American Scholar*, Spring, pp. 173-84.

Berger, Bennet M. 1957. "Sociology and the Intellectuals," *Antioch Review*, Fall, pp. 275-90.

Birnbaum, Norman. 1958. "America, a Partial View," *Commentary*, July, pp. 42-47.

Borkenau, Franz. 1951. "Will Technology Destroy Civilization?" trans. by Martin Greenberg, *Commentary*, January, pp. 20-26.

Braybrooke, David. 1958. "Diagnosis and Remedy in Marx's Doctrine of Alienation," *Social Research*, Autumn, pp. 325-45.

Burnham, Jas. 1950. "The Suicidal Mania of American Business," *Partisan Review*, January, pp. 47-63.

Bush, Douglas. 1959. "The Real Maladjustment," *Harvard Foundation Newsletter*, September 30, pp. 1-3.

Chase, Richard. 1955. "Is There a Middle Way in Culture?" *Commentary*, July, pp. 57-63.

———. 1957a. "Heresy and Modern Culture," *Dissent*, Spring, pp. 128-32.

———. 1957b. "The Fate of the Avant-garde," *Partisan Review*, Summer, pp. 363-75.

Chiaromonte, Nicola. 1957. "The Individual and the Mass," *Dissent*, Spring, pp. 167-77.

Childe, Gordon. 1954. *What Happened in History*. Rev. ed. Baltimore: Penguin Books.

Cohen, Arthur A. 1956. "Religion as a Secular Ideology," *Partisan Review*, Fall, pp. 495-505.

Cohn, David L. 1949a. "Moonlight and Poison Ivy," *Atlantic Monthly*, January, pp. 36-38.

———. 1949b. "Who Will Do the Dirty Work?" *Atlantic Monthly*, May, pp. 45-48.

References

Cooley, Charles Horton. 1902. *Human Nature and the Social Order*. New York: Chas. Scribner's Sons.

Coser, Lewis. 1956a. *The Functions of Social Conflict*. Glencoe: The Free Press.

————. 1956b. "What Shall We Do?" *Dissent*, Spring, pp. 156-65.

————. 1957. "Portraits and Profiles," *Dissent*, Summer, pp. 210-13.

————. 1958. "Nightmares, Daydreams, and Prof. Shils," *Dissent*, Summer, pp. 268-73.

Cronin, Martin. 1958. "The American Intellectual," *American Association of University Professors Bulletin*, Summer, pp. 403-15.

Crossland, C. A. R. 1958. "Land of Plenty," *Partisan Review*, Fall, pp. 613-19.

cummings, e. e. 1953a. "i & my parents' son," *Atlantic Monthly*, April, pp. 57-62.

————. 1953b. "i & self-discovery," *Atlantic Monthly*, May, pp. 53-58.

Denney, Reuel, 1951. "Hail, Meeters! Greeters, Farewell," *Commentary*, October, pp. 382-87.

Durkheim, Emile. 1949. *The Division of Labor in Society*. Trans. by George Simpson. Glencoe: The Free Press.

Eliot, T. S. 1948. *Notes Towards the Definition of Culture*. London: Faber and Faber.

Emerson, R. W. secundus [pseudonym]. 1950. "Television's Peril to Culture," *American Scholar*, Spring, pp. 137-40.

Erikson, Erik H. 1950. *Childhood and Society*. New York: W. W. Norton.

Fitch, Robert E. 1953. "The Illusions of the Intelligentsia," *Commentary*, December, pp. 562-67.

Flanders, Ralph E. 1951. "How Big Is an Inch?" *Atlantic Monthly*, January, pp. 44-48.

Fortune, Editors of. 1955. *The Changing American Market*. Garden City: Hanover House.

Freud, Sigmund. 1955. *Civilization and Its Discontents*. Trans. by Joan Riviere. London: The Hogarth Press.

Fromm, Erich. 1947. *Man for Himself*. New York: Rinehart.

————. 1954. "The Psychology of Normalcy," *Dissent*, Spring, pp. 139-43.

————. 1955a. "The Human Implications of Instinctivistic 'Radicalism,'" *Dissent*, Autumn, pp. 342-49.

————. 1955b. *The Sane Society*. New York: Rinehart.

————. 1955-56. "The Present Human Condition," *American Scholar*, Winter, pp. 29-35.

Galbraith, John Kenneth. 1958. *The Affluent Society*. Boston: Houghton Mifflin.

Gans, Herbert J. 1958. "Popular Culture and High Culture Critics," *Dissent*, Spring, pp. 185-87.

Geertz, Clifford. 1957. "A Theory of Political Ideology and Its Application to the American and Indonesian Cases." Unpublished seminar paper, Harvard.

Glick, Paul C. 1957. *American Families*. A volume in the census monograph series. New York: John Wiley and Sons.

Gold, Herbert. 1957. "The Age of Happy Problems," *Atlantic Monthly*, March, pp. 58-61.

Greenberg, Clement. 1953a. "The Plight of Our Culture," *Commentary*, June, pp. 558-66.

————. 1953b. "Work and Leisure under Industrialism," *Commentary*, July, pp. 54-61.

H. P. 1956. "The Insane Society," *Dissent*, Winter, pp. 84-89.

Handlin, Oscar. 1949. "Group Life within the American Pattern," *Commentary*, November, pp. 411-17.

————. 1951. "Yearning for Security," *Atlantic Monthly*, January, pp. 25-27.

————. 1953. "Payroll Prosperity," *Atlantic Monthly*, February, pp. 29-33.

————. 1955. "Does the People's Rule Doom Democracy?" *Commentary*, July, pp. 1-7.

Hatt, Paul K., and Albert J. Riess, Jr., eds. 1951. *Reader in Urban Sociology*. Glencoe: The Free Press.

Hauser, Arnold. 1958. "Popular Art and Folk Art," *Dissent*, Summer, pp. 229-37.

Hausknecht, Murray. 1957. "The Mike in the Bosom," *Dissent*, Winter, pp. 56-59.

Heinemann, F. H. 1958. *Existentialism and the Modern Predicament*. New York: Harper & Bros.

Herberg, Will. 1955. "America's New Religiousness," *Commentary*, September, pp. 240-47.

Hicks, Granville. 1953. "How We Live Now in America," *Commentary*, December, pp. 505-12.

——. 1956. "Liberalism in the Fifties," *American Scholar,* Summer, pp. 283-96.

Howe, Irving. 1954a. "Stevenson and the Intellectuals," *Dissent,* Winter, pp. 12-21.

——. 1954b. "This Age of Conformity," *Partisan Review,* January-February, pp. 7-33.

——. 1955. "America, the Country and the Myth," *Dissent,* Summer, pp. 241-44.

Hughes, Stuart H. 1956. "Is the Intellectual Obsolete?" *Commentary,* October, pp. 313-19.

Huxley, Aldous. 1932. *Brave New World.* New York: Harper & Bros.

Jarrell, Randall. 1952. "The Age of Criticism," *Partisan Review,* March-April, pp. 185-201 .

Jaspers, Karl. 1950. "Is Science Evil?" *Commentary,* March, pp. 229-33.

Johnson, Miriam Massey. 1955. *Instrumental and Expressive Components in the Personalities of Women.* Unpublished doctoral dissertation, Radcliffe.

Kaplan, David L., and M. Claire Casey. 1958. *Occupational Trends in the United States, 1900 to 1950.* U.S. Dept. of Commerce, Bureau of the Census.

Kazin, Alfred. 1958. "John P. Marquand and the American Failure," *Atlantic Monthly,* November, pp. 152-56.

Kecskemeti, Paul. 1956. "The All-powerful 'I,' " *Commentary,* February, pp. 176-79.

Kelman, Norman. 1955. "Psychoanalysis and Morality," *American Scholar,* Spring, pp. 158-70.

Klonsky, Milton. 1949. "Along the Midway of Mass Culture," *Partisan Review,* April, pp. 348-65.

Kluckhohn, Clyde. 1952. "Values and Value-Orientations in the Theory of Action," in *Toward a General Theory of Action,* ed. by Talcott Parsons and Edward A. Shils. Cambridge: Harvard University Press.

——. 1958. "Have There Been Discernible Shifts in American Values during the Past Generation?" in *The American Style,* ed. by Elting E. Morison. New York: Harper & Bros.

Kolko, Gabriel. 1957. "American 'Income Revolution,' " *Dissent,* Winter, pp. 35-55.

Kornhauser, William. 1959. *The Politics of Mass Society.* Glencoe: The Free Press.

Kramer, Hilton. 1956. "In Search of Heresy," *Partisan Review*, Fall, pp. 553-56.

Kroeber, A. L., and Talcott Parsons. 1958. "The Concepts of Culture and of Social System," *American Sociological Review*, October, pp. 582-83.

Kronenberger, Louis. 1951-52. "The Spirit of Our Age," *American Scholar*, Winter, pp. 10-20.

———. 1953. "America and Art," *American Scholar*, Autumn, pp. 399-408.

Krutch, Joseph Wood. 1950. "Freedom for Radio and TV?" *Commentary*, November, pp. 434-38.

———. 1953. "The Loss of Confidence," *American Scholar*, Spring, pp. 141-53.

———. 1955-56. "If you don't mind my saying so . . ." *American Scholar*, Winter, 1955-56, pp. 80-86.

———. 1956. "If you don't mind my saying so . . ." *American Scholar*, Autumn, 468-71.

Kuznets, Simon. 1946. *National Income: A Summary of Findings*. New York: National Bureau of Economic Research.

Lamont, Corliss. 1949. *Humanism as a Philosophy*. 3rd ed. New York: Philosophical Library.

Lekachman, Robert. 1957. "Organization Men," *Commentary*, March, pp. 270-76.

Lerner, Daniel. 1958. "Comfort and Fun: Morality in a Nice Society," *American Scholar*, Spring, pp. 153-65.

Lerner, Max. 1955-56. "The Flowering of Latter-Day Man," *American Scholar*, Winter, pp. 21-27.

———. 1957. *America as a Civilization*. New York: Simon and Schuster.

Lipset, Seymour. 1960. *Political Man: The Social Bases of Politics*. Garden City: Doubleday.

Livingstone, Sir Richard. 1953. "The Meaning of Civilization," *Atlantic Monthly*, March, pp. 39-44.

Lottman, Michael. 1960. "The Secret of Freedom" [a review of MacLeish's television play], *The Harvard Crimson*, March 1, p. 2.

Lynd, Helen M., 1951-52. "Realism and the Intellectual," *American Scholar*, Winter, pp. 21-32.

Lynes, Russell. 1949. "Highbrow, Lowbrow, Middlebrow," *Harper's*, February, pp. 19-28.

Macdonald, Dwight. 1957. "A Theory of Mass Culture," in Rosenberg and White, eds., *Mass Culture, q.v.*

———. 1958a. "America! America!" *Dissent*, Autumn, pp. 313-23.

———. 1958b. "The Lost Art," *New Yorker*, March 15, pp. 121-42.

MacLeish, Archibald. 1949. "The Conquest of America," *Atlantic Monthly*, August, pp. 17-22.

———. 1950. "The American State of Mind," *American Scholar*, Autumn, pp. 398-408.

———. 1951a. "The Power of Choice," *Atlantic Monthly*, August, pp. 41-44.

———. 1951b. "To Make Men Free," *Atlantic Monthly*, November, pp. 27-30.

———. 1953. "Loyalty and Freedom," *American Scholar*, Autumn, pp. 393-98.

———. 1956. "Why We Teach Poetry," *Atlantic Monthly*, March, pp. 48-53.

———. 1958. "The Isolation of the American Artist," *Atlantic Monthly*, January, pp. 55-59.

Mailer, Norman. 1954. "David Riesman Reconsidered," *Dissent*, Autumn, pp. 349-59.

———. 1957. "The White Negro," *Dissent*, Summer, pp. 276-93.

Mandel, Oscar. 1958. "Nobility and the United States,'" *American Scholar*, Spring, pp. 197-212.

Mann, Golo. 1950. "The American Credo Survives the Modern Crisis," *Commentary*, April, pp. 301-07.

Mannheim, Karl. 1936. *Ideology and Utopia*. Trans. by Louis Wirth and Edward Shils. New York: Harcourt, Brace.

Marcuse, Herbert. 1955a. *Eros and Civilization*. Boston: Beacon Press.

———. 1955b. "The Social Implications of Freudian Revisionism," *Dissent*, Summer, pp. 221-40.

———, and Erich Fromm. 1956. [An exchange], *Dissent*, Winter, pp. 79-83.

Marcuse, Ludwig. 1952. "The Oldest Younger Generation," *Partisan Review*, March-April, pp. 211-16.

Marx, Walter. 1949. "Technology and Disintegration," *Commonweal*, July 29, pp. 391-93.

McClelland, David C., John W. Atkinson, Russell A. Clark, and Edgar A. Lowell. 1953. *The Achievement Motive*. New York: Appleton-Century-Crofts.

McKitrick, Eric L. 1957-58. " 'Conservatism' Today," *American Scholar*, Winter, pp. 49-61.

McLuhan, Marshall. 1957. "American Advertising," in Rosenberg and White, eds., *Mass Culture*, *q.v.*

Mead, Margaret. 1956. "Our Documentary Culture," *American Scholar*, Autumn, pp. 401-09.

Meserve, Harry C. 1955. "The New Piety," *Atlantic Monthly*, June, pp. 34-37.

Miller, Herman P. 1955. *Income of the American People*. New York: John Wiley and Sons.

Miller, Perry. 1956. "The Plight of the Lone Wolf," *American Scholar*, Autumn, pp. 445-51.

Mills, C. Wright. 1951. *White Collar: The American Middle Classes*. New York: Oxford University Press.

———. 1954. "The Conservative Mood," *Dissent*, Winter, pp. 23-31.

———. 1956. *The Power Elite*. New York: Oxford University Press.

Muhlen, Norbert. 1949. "Comic Books and Other Horrors," *Commentary*, January, pp. 80-87.

Neumann, William L. 1957. "Historians in an Age of Acquiescence," *Dissent*, Winter, pp. 64-69.

Newman, William J. 1956. "The Importance of Being Radical," *Dissent*, Spring, pp. 165-70.

———. 1957. "Americans in Subtopia," *Dissent*, Summer, pp. 255-66.

Niebuhr, Reinhold. 1944. *Children of Light and Children of Darkness*. New York: Chas. Scribner's Sons.

———. 1952. *The Irony of American History*. New York: Chas. Scribner's Sons.

———. 1955-56. "The Cause and Cure of the American Psychosis," *American Scholar*, Winter, pp. 11-20.

Ortega y Gasset, José. 1950. *The Revolt of the Masses*. Anonymous trans. New York: Mentor Books.

Orwell, George. 1949. *1984*. New York: Harcourt, Brace.

Packard, Vance. 1957. "The Growing Power of Admen," *Atlantic Monthly*, September, pp. 55-59.

———. 1958. "Public Relations: Good or Bad," *Atlantic Monthly*, May, pp. 53-57.

Parkes, Henry Bamford. 1951. "Gyroscope and Radar," *Partisan Review*, January-February, pp. 114-19.

——. 1956. "The Reformer as Reactionary," *Partisan Review*, Spring, pp. 274-78.

Parsons, Talcott. 1949. *The Structure of Social Action*. Glencoe: The Free Press.

——. 1951. *The Social System*. Glencoe: The Free Press.

——. 1958. "Social Structure and the Development of Personality," *Psychiatry*, November, pp. 321-40.

——. 1959a. "Comments on 'American Intellectuals: Their Politics and Status,'" *Daedalus*, Summer, pp. 493-95.

——. 1959b. "Some Problems Confronting Sociology as a Profession," *American Sociological Review*, August, pp. 547-59.

——. 1960. *Structure and Process in Modern Societies*. Glencoe: The Free Press.

——. 1961. "An Approach to the Sociology of Knowledge," in *Proceedings of the Fourth World Congress of Sociology*, ed. by Kurt Wolff. To be published.

——, Edward Shils, Kaspar D. Naegele, and Jesse R. Pitts, eds. 1961. *Theories of Society*. 2 vols. Glencoe: The Free Press.

——, and Winston White. 1961. "The Link between Character and Society," in *Culture and Social Character: The Work of David Riesman Reviewed*, ed. by Seymour Lipset and Leo Lowenthal. Glencoe: The Free Press.

Partisan Review Symposium. 1952a. "Our Country and Our Culture," May-June, pp. 282-326.

——. 1952b. "Our Country and Our Culture," July-August, pp. 420-50.

——. 1952c. "Our Country and Our Culture," September-October, pp. 562-97.

Podhoretz, Norman. 1953. "Our Changing Ideals, As Seen on TV," *Commentary*, December, pp. 534-40.

Rabasseire, Henri. 1956a. "Some Aspects of Mass Culture," *Dissent*, Summer, pp. 327-32.

——. 1956b. "The Right to be Lazy," *Dissent*, Winter, pp. 37-44.

——. 1957. "What Price Work?" *Dissent*, Autumn, pp. 421-27.

——. 1958. "Confessions of an Old-Timer," *Dissent*, Winter, pp. 32-42.

Rabi, I. I. 1956. "Scientist and Humanist," *Atlantic Monthly*, January, pp. 64-67.

Rawick, George. 1954. "The American Student: A Profile," *Dissent*, Autumn, pp. 393-98.

Ray, Arthur. 1955. "Science: From the 'Bomb' to . . . ?" *Dissent*, Winter, pp. 66-70.

Reagan, Michael. 1956. "America as a 'Mass Society,'" *Dissent*, Fall, pp. 346-56.

Richter, Conrad. 1950. "That Early American Quality," *Atlantic Monthly*, September, pp. 26-30.

Rieff, Philip. 1956. "Socialism and Sociology," *Partisan Review*, Summer, pp. 365-69.

―――. 1957. "A Character Wrecked by Success," *Partisan Review*, Spring, pp. 304-10.

Riesman, David (in collaboration with Reuel Denney and Nathan Glazer). 1950. *The Lonely Crowd: A Study of the Changing American Character*. New Haven: Yale University Press.

―――. 1953-54. "Some Observations on Intellectual Freedom," *American Scholar*, Winter, pp. 9-25.

―――. 1954. *Individualism Reconsidered and Other Essays*. Glencoe: The Free Press.

―――. 1956. "The Found Generation," *American Scholar*, Autumn, pp. 421-36.

―――, and Nathan Glazer. 1955. "The Intellectuals and the Discontented Classes," *Partisan Review*, Winter, pp. 47-72.

Riley, John W., Jr., and Matilda White Riley. 1959. "Mass Communication and the Social System," in *Sociology Today*, ed. by Robert K. Merton, Leonard Broom, and Leonard S. Cottrell, Jr. New York: Basic Books.

Rogow, Arnold A. 1957. "The Revolt against Social Equality," *Dissent*, Autumn, pp. 365-71.

Rosenberg, Bernard. 1953. "Social Science and the Humanists," *American Scholar*, Spring, pp. 203-14.

―――. 1954. "The Economics of Self-Congratulation," *Dissent*, Winter, pp. 92-102.

―――. 1956. "Attitudes to Mass Culture," *Dissent*, Winter, pp. 25-28.

―――. 1957. "Mass Culture in America," in Rosenberg and White, eds., *Mass Culture. q.v.*

―――. 1958. "Rebellious Orgmen and Tame Intellectuals," *Dissent*, Spring, pp. 119-24.

———, and David Manning White, eds. 1957. *Mass Culture.* Glencoe: The Free Press.

Rosenberg, Harold. 1956. "Marxism: Criticism and/or Action," *Dissent*, Fall, pp. 366-75.

———. 1958a. "Twilight of the Intellectuals," *Dissent*, Summer, pp. 221-28.

———. 1958b. "Pop Culture and Kitsch Criticism," *Dissent*, Winter, pp. 14-19.

Rosenthal, M. L., 1951. "The Professors Cling to their Faith," *Commentary*, September, pp. 275-77.

Rostow, W. W. 1960. *The Stages of Economic Growth.* New York: Cambridge University Press.

Rovere, Richard H. 1958. "The Invasion of Privacy: Technology and the Claims of Community," *American Scholar*, Autumn, pp. 413-21.

Rowland, Stanley J., Jr. 1958. "Religion and the Younger Generation," *American Scholar*, Summer, pp. 299-306.

Russell, Bertrand. 1949. "The Exceptional Man," *Atlantic Monthly*, November, pp. 52-56.

Sapir, Edward. 1949. "Culture, Genuine and Spurious," in *Selected Writings of Edward Sapir*, ed. by David G. Mandelbaum. Berkeley: University of California Press.

Schlesinger, Arthur, Jr. 1953. "The Highbrow in American Politics," *Partisan Review*, March-April, pp. 156-65.

Seiden, Melvin. 1958. "Cancer in the U.S.: An Extended Metaphor," *Dissent*, Summer, pp. 274-78.

Seligman, Ben B. 1957. "Ideology and Big Business," *Dissent*, Autumn, pp. 372-75.

Shahn, Ben. 1957. "Nonconformity," *Atlantic Monthly*, September, pp. 36-41.

Shils, Edward. 1957. "Daydreams and Nightmares," *Sewanee Review*, Autumn, pp. 587-608.

———. 1958. "The Intellectuals and the Powers: Some Perspectives for Comparative Analysis," *Comparative Studies in Society and History*, October, pp. 5-22.

Shklar, Judith N. 1957. *After Utopia.* Princeton: Princeton University Press.

Skinner, B. F. 1955-56. "Freedom and the Control of Men," *American Scholar*, Winter, pp. 47-65.

Snow, C. P. 1959. *The Two Cultures and the Scientific Revolution.* New York: Cambridge University Press.

Speyer, Edward. 1957. "Scientists in the Bureaucratic Age," *Dissent*, Autumn, pp. 402-13.

Stein, Maurice. 1957. "Suburbia—a Walk on the Mild Side," *Dissent*, Summer, pp. 267-75.

Stouffer, Samuel A. 1955. *Communism, Conformity, and Civil Liberties.* Garden City: Doubleday.

Strunsky, Robert. 1956. "The Cult of Personality," *American Scholar*, Summer, pp. 265-72.

Sutton, Francis X., Seymour E. Harris, Carl Kaysen, and James Tobin. 1956. *The American Business Creed.* Cambridge: Harvard University Press.

Swados, Harvey. 1954. "Popular Music and the New Man of Skill," *Dissent*, Summer, pp. 269-73.

———. 1956. "Exurbia Revisited," *Dissent*, Spring, pp. 203-06.

———. 1958. "Popular Taste and the Agonies of the Young," *Dissent*, Spring, pp. 174-77.

Thompson, Lovell. 1951. "Progress and Decline," *Atlantic Monthly*, June, pp. 53-58.

Tocqueville, Alexis de. 1957. *Democracy in America.* 2 vols. New York: Knopf.

Troeltsch, Ernst. 1931. *The Social Teaching of the Christian Churches.* 2 vols. Trans. by Olive Wyon. New York: Macmillan.

Van den Haag, Ernest. 1957. "Of Happiness and Despair We Have No Measure," in Rosenberg and White, eds., *Mass Culture, q.v.*

Viereck, Peter. 1949. "Conservatism Revisited," *Atlantic Monthly*, August, pp. 60-68.

Walter, Eugene Victor. 1955. "The Chimera of Conservatism," *Dissent*, Summer, pp. 250-56.

———. 1956. "The Masses and the Elite," *Dissent*, Winter, pp. 75-78.

Ward, Barbara. 1951. "The Silent Revolution," *Atlantic Monthly*, July, pp. 34-38.

Weber, Max. 1946. *From Max Weber: Essays in Sociology.* Trans., ed., and intro. by H. H. Gerth and C. Wright Mills. New York: Oxford University Press.

References   [225]

————. 1958. *The Protestant Ethic and the Spirit of Capitalism.*
    Trans. by Talcott Parsons. New York: Chas. Scribner's
    Sons.
Weeks, Edward. 1958. "How Big Is One?" *Atlantic Monthly*,
    August, pp. 25-30.
Wheeler, Harvey. 1957. "Danger Signals in the Political System,"
    Dissent, Summer, pp. 298-310.
Wheeler, Robert. 1956-57. "Mr. Riesman's Consumers," *Ameri-
    can Scholar*, Winter, pp. 39-50.
Wheelis, Allen. 1958. *The Quest for Identity.* New York: W. W.
    Norton.
Whyte, William H., Jr. 1956. *The Organization Man.* Garden
    City: Doubleday.
Wrong, Dennis H. 1950. "The 'Break-up' of the American Fam-
    ily," *Commentary*, April, pp. 374-80.
————. 1956. "Riesman and the Age of Sociology," *Commentary*,
    April, pp. 331-34.
Yellen, Samuel. 1950. "The Statisdemon," *Commentary*, July,
    pp. 81-83.

U. S. Government Publications

Bureau of the Census. 1957. *Current Population Report, P50, No.*
    71, "Employment of Students: October 1956."
————. 1959a. *Statistical Abstract of the United States 1959.*
————. 1959b. *Current Population Report, P20, No. 93,* "School
    Enrolment."
Bureau of Labor Statistics. 1959. "Increase in the Scientific, Engi-
    neering, and Other Technical Jobs," *Occupational Outlook
    Quarterly* (February).
Office of Business Economics. 1958. *U. S. Income and Output.*

Index